FREDERICK DOUGLASS
IN BROOKLYN

BY FREDERICK DOUGLASS

EDITED BY
THEODORE HAMM

Published by Akashic Books
Theodore Hamm's introduction, annotations, and additional text ©2017

Portions of Chapter Four, "Emancipation Jubilee," appeared in *Jacobin* in August 2015. Reprinted by permission of publisher.

Cover photograph of Frederick Douglass: Augustus Morand, May 15, 1863. *Carte-de-visite* (2-1/2" x 4"), Lynn Museum and Historical Society, Hutchinson Family Singers Album. Taken before a speech at the Brooklyn Academy of Music.

Cover illustration: *Brooklyn, L.I., as Seen from Trinity Church, New York, painted by J.W. Hill; Smith, Brors. del.* New York: Published by Smith Brothers & Co., 225 Fulton St., 1853. Image retrieved from the Library of Congress Prints and Photographs Division, https://www.loc.gov/item/2014645205/.

ISBN: 978-1-61775-485-2
Library of Congress Control Number: 2016935081

Akashic Books
Twitter: @AkashicBooks
Facebook: AkashicBooks
E-mail: info@akashicbooks.com
Website: www.akashicbooks.com

For Toni and Ellis

TABLE OF CONTENTS

Frederick Douglass, a man born in bondage and committed to the freedom of his people, arrived in Brooklyn to share a message of equality at institutions we know today, such as Bridge Street African Methodist Episcopal Church in Bedford-Stuyvesant and Plymouth Church in Brooklyn Heights. His descriptions of the evils of slavery resounded in the ears of listeners, and his speeches inspired their work as abolitionists. We continue to honor his legacy with three Frederick Douglass Academy schools in Brooklyn. It is my hope that this book will introduce Mr. Douglass to a generation that could benefit from the example of his clarity of purpose and moral vision, as well as his relationship to the Borough of Brooklyn.

—BROOKLYN BOROUGH PRESIDENT ERIC L. ADAMS

INTRODUCTION

Mr. Douglass has been in the habit of carrying his audiences by storm. His peculiar wit, sarcasm, drollery, dramatic intensity, and, more than all, his noble moral earnestness, set in strong relief by an indefinable and touching sadness of tone and mien, [are] apparent [in] all his speeches. Though he makes his listeners alternately cheer, laugh, and weep, they inevitably carry away with them, as the chief impression of the evening, not the ornament or side-play, but the logical frame-work and solid sense of the discourse. Frederick Douglass, beginning his life as a bond-slave, will leave behind him an honest fame as one of the chief orators of his day and generation.
—*Brooklyn's Theodore Tilton*, Independent, *February 12, 1863*

Upon Frederick Douglass's death in 1895, the *New York Tribune*—a newspaper founded by a leading abolitionist, Horace Greeley—dug up a chestnut from a half-century earlier. In 1846, Douglass had delivered a speech at a temperance gathering in London's Covent Garden Theatre. There he told an audience that included both British royalty and US ministers that while temperance was indeed a worthy cause, the abolition of slavery was more important. After Douglass's address, the *Tribune* said, among those who sought to congratulate the speaker was an "eminent Brooklyn divine." Never one to mince words, Douglass rejected the overture. He told the minister, "Sir, were we to have met under similar circumstances in Brooklyn, you would never have ventured to take my hand, and you shall not do it here."[1]

Beyond illustrating Douglass's resolute character, the anecdote also yields insight into Brooklyn's race relations in the decades before the Civil War. Despite the presence of prominent white abolitionists, as well as that of vocal African Americans, Brooklyn was far from a haven of black equality. In the wake of the London meeting, Douglass engaged in a high-profile war of words in print with Reverend Samuel Hanson Cox, the prominent pastor of Brooklyn's First Presbyterian Church. Though an abolitionist, Cox was outraged that Douglass had raised the issue of slavery at the temperance convention. In the *New York Evangelist*, a Presbyterian weekly newspaper, Cox called Douglass's actions a "perversion" of the meeting's intent and "abominable!" In William Lloyd Garrison's *Liberator*, an influential abolitionist paper from Boston, Douglass labeled Cox a "sham" opponent of slavery. Audiences across the Northeast thus became aware of Brooklyn's contested racial terrain.[2]

---

1 *New York Tribune*, February 21, 1895.
2 The New York Anti-Slavery Society published a pamphlet of the exchange in

Frederick Douglass never lived in Brooklyn, but his visits to the "City of Churches" stirred both enthusiasm and controversy. During the Civil War era many of his key friends and allies—including Henry Ward Beecher, Theodore Tilton, Lewis Tappan, James and Elizabeth Gloucester, James McCune Smith, and William J. Wilson (a.k.a. "Ethiop")—called Brooklyn home. Douglass had close ties to three publications with Brooklyn roots: the *Ram's Horn* (1847–1849), the *Anglo-African* (1859–1865), and the *Independent* (1860s). Meanwhile, his own publications, the *North Star* and *Frederick Douglass' Paper*, featured regular Brooklyn correspondents, most notably Ethiop. Douglass was a close friend of John Brown, and the pages of the *Anglo-African* noted the former's stop in Brooklyn—at the home of Elizabeth Gloucester—en route to a pivotal Harpers Ferry planning meeting in late August 1859. Theodore Tilton, who rose to prominence in his defense of Brown in the *Independent*, would become one of Douglass's closest confidants during the Civil War and Reconstruction.

Both in person and print, Douglass was a powerful presence in Brooklyn—and the varied reactions to his positions on abolition and black equality thus illustrate the ways in which those issues shaped the city in its formative decades. At African American churches like

---

1846. Over the next decade, Douglass maintained the feud in his publications. It's likely that Cox, who attended the Covent Garden meeting, is the "Brooklyn divine" in the *Tribune* anecdote.

Reverend James N. Gloucester's Siloam Presbyterian or James Morris Williams's Bridge Street AME, or at white abolitionist strongholds like Henry Ward Beecher's Plymouth Church, the gifted orator received a hero's welcome. But in the pages of the *Brooklyn Daily Eagle*, a conservative Democratic organ during the Civil War, Douglass was often subjected to racist ridicule. Douglass had garnered a more friendly reception from Walt Whitman, during the latter's short stints as editor of both the *Eagle* and the *Brooklyn Daily Times*. Even so, Whitman's position on racial issues—antislavery but not proequality—reflected a notable current of local sentiment. Like New York City, Brooklyn (its own city until 1898) had strong economic ties to Southern slavery, making the place a racial minefield. But with the help of his steadfast allies, Douglass navigated it safely.

Twenty-year-old Frederick Bailey first became acquainted with New York abolitionists in September 1838. Born a slave on the Eastern Shore of Maryland around February 1818, Bailey came of age in Baltimore, where he learned to read and soon inspired his peers to do the same; after a few unsuccessful attempts to escape, he fled safely to New York via trains and ferries while carrying the identification papers of a free black seaman. Once in Manhattan, Bailey sought out David Ruggles, a leading African American conductor of the Underground Railroad. He informed Ruggles of his desire to marry his fiancée, Anna Murray, who would soon join him in New York; soon thereafter, Reverend James W.C. Pennington came from Brooklyn to perform the wedding at Ruggles's home on Lispenard Street. (Thus began a long alliance between the soon-to-be Douglass and Pennington—who would preside over Shiloh Presbyterian, an abolitionist stronghold on Prince Street in Manhattan.) From New York, Frederick and Anna traveled via boat to Newport, Rhode Island, then by stagecoach to New Bedford, Massachusetts, where they set up shop and became the Douglass family. In the summer of 1841, Douglass first met William Lloyd Garrison, who helped launch his career as a public figure. That fall, the family moved to Lynn, Massachusetts, and it was there that Douglass wrote the book that would build his international reputation, *Narrative of the Life of Frederick Douglass, an American Slave*, which Garrison's American Anti-Slavery Society published in 1845.

Brooklyn was far from a bastion of abolitionist support in the mid-1840s. Many early Kings County residents had owned slaves, and after Brooklyn officially became a city in 1834, local merchants competed with their counterparts across the East River for the trade in Southern products. Indeed, so widespread was the support for slavery in Brooklyn that in 1839 David Ruggles called the city "the Savannah of New York."[3] Beginning

3 See Graham Russell Hodges, *David Ruggles: A Radical Black Abolitionist and the Underground Railroad in New York City* (Chapel Hill, NC: University of North

in May 1842, Douglass spoke at the annual meetings of the Garrison-led American Anti-Slavery Society in Manhattan, which usually took place at the Broadway Tabernacle, the church where the Tappan brothers held sway. Beyond abolitionist circles, Douglass was not a household name in the New York area until his autobiography came out—and even then Brooklyn audiences more likely read about him in Horace Greeley's *New York Tribune* (which published a front-page review by Margaret Fuller in June 1845) than in any local publication. Douglass, in turn, spent the next two years touring Ireland and England. Among his fellow speakers at the August 1846 temperance convention in London was Henry Ward Beecher, the charismatic Congregationalist minister who moved the following year from Indiana to Brooklyn, where he became the first pastor of Plymouth Church. Beecher's arrival meant that Douglass and his fellow abolitionists in Brooklyn now had a much more sympathetic ally than Samuel Cox.

Upon his return from England in the spring of 1847, Douglass informed his colleagues that he planned to start his own publication. He was still based in Lynn, but sought independence from Garrison, who presided over Boston-area abolitionists. Throughout 1847, various reports placed Douglass's publication in different

Carolina Press, 2010), 144.

locations, including Lynn, Cleveland, and Rochester, its eventual home. One of the earliest announcements came from Walt Whitman, who had been editing the *Brooklyn Daily Eagle* for just over a year. In early June of 1847, Whitman noted:

> *Fred. Douglass, the runaway slave, having received the necessary subscriptions and contributions for a press etc., from Scotland principally, is about to publish an anti-slavery paper in Lynn, Mass. He will of course create a great sensation in the regions around shoe-dom. A Sunday paper says that Lynn and the neighboring peninsula of Nahant have heretofore mainly depended for excitement on the appearance of the sea serpent, whose visits of late years have been singularly irregular. Douglass will prove a first-rate substitute for the monster.*[4]

Playful but clearly supportive, Whitman's statement was based on word that spread in the wake of the May annual meeting of the American Anti-Slavery Society at the Broadway Tabernacle, where Douglass had spoken. There is no record of the two figures formally meeting one another, but at the time Whitman and Douglass were traveling in similar circles—and the former's op-

---

4 *Brooklyn Daily Eagle*, June 4, 1847.

position to slavery would cause him to lose his job at the *Eagle* in early 1848.

As he prepared to launch his own paper, Douglass also became involved with the *Ram's Horn*, which was published by Willis Hodges, a leading figure in the black community in Williamsburgh (as it was spelled at the time), which would not become part of Brooklyn until 1855. The *Ram's Horn* debuted in January 1847, with Thomas Van Rensselaer, a former slave turned Manhattan restaurateur, as its editor. Hodges, who became close friends with John Brown, had owned a small grocery stand near the ferry in Williamsburgh, and his brother William was also a leading minister in the area. After the May meeting of the Anti-Slavery Society, Douglass wrote to van Rensselaer, encouraging him to "Blow away on your 'Ram's Horn'! Its wild, rough, uncultivated notes may grate harshly on the ear of [the] refined . . . but sure I am that its voice will be pleasurable to the slave, and terrible to the slaveholder."[5] In early August 1847, the paper announced that Douglass had joined the masthead as an assistant editor; Sydney Howard Gay, editor of the *National Anti-Slavery Standard* (also based in Manhattan), confirmed that report, adding that Douglass would also serve as a regular contributor to the *Standard*. Douglass, in turn, asked Gay to look into the *Horn*'s finances, in order to make sure he wouldn't

5 Letter, May 18, 1847, from *Frederick Douglass: Selected Speeches and Writings*, Philip S. Foner and Yuval Taylor, eds. (Chicago Review Press, 1999), 83–85.

incur any debts.[6] For the next several months, Douglass remained affiliated with the *Ram's Horn*.

In the fall of 1847, African American audiences on both sides of the East River could thus read a weekly paper that featured Frederick Douglass on its masthead. The banner across page one of the only extant copy of the *Ram's Horn*—dated November 5, 1847—lists Van Rensselaer and Douglass as editors, placing their names on opposite sides of the paper's motto: *We are Men—and therefore interested in whatever concerns Men*. It's not clear what Douglass actually contributed to this (or any other) issue, but the editorial page carried his name in the top left-hand corner. Under it was a signed editorial from Willis Hodges encouraging readers to take interest in the "Gerrit Smith Lands." Smith was a prominent abolitionist from Western New York who encouraged blacks (and white abolitionists) to become farmers on the 120,000 acres he donated to a community called "Timbuctoo" in North Elba, near Lake Placid. In the fall of 1848, Hodges became one of several New York City–area migrants to Timbuctoo, where fellow resident John Brown (a *Ram's Horn* contributor) helped him set up shop.[7] Gerrit Smith, meanwhile, would become a

---

6 Letter, August 13, 1847, from *The Frederick Douglass Papers: 1842–1852,* John R. McKivigan, ed., Series 3, Vol. 1 (New Haven, CT: Yale University Press, 2009), 227–228.

7 Brown's letter to Hodges (October 28, 1848) is featured in the Brooklyn Historical Society's exhibition about abolitionism in Brooklyn (pursuitoffreedom. org). For a discussion of Brown's controversial *Ram's Horn* essay, "Sambo's Mistakes"

pivotal supporter of both Douglass's own paper as well as Brown's raid on Harpers Ferry. In 1849, Van Rensselaer moved the *Ram's Horn* to Philadelphia, where it fizzled out a year later.

That same November 1847 issue of the *Ram's Horn* also carried an announcement informing readers that contrary to recent reports, Douglass planned to publish his own paper in Rochester, not Cleveland.[8] One month later, the *North Star* indeed made its debut from the city on the banks of Lake Ontario that Douglass would call home for the next twenty-three years. In his inaugural statement, Douglass declared, "It has long been our anxious wish to see . . . [a paper] under the complete control and direction of the immediate victims of slavery and oppression."[9] That jab seemed directed at Garrison and the *Liberator*, because it didn't apply to the *Ram's Horn* (or other preceding black-edited newspapers). But in order to sustain the *North Star*, Douglass needed to raise a steady stream of funds, via both donations and subscriptions. While Gerrit Smith was a steady source of financial support, according to biographer William McFeely, over the next few years, "Everywhere he went,

---

(in which the writer criticized free blacks for pursuing material comforts rather than fight for abolition), see Reynolds, *John Brown, Abolitionist* (New York: Vintage, 2006), 119–121.

8 The October 15, 1847, issue of the *Liberator* carried Douglass's "Prospectus for the North Star," the first line of which read, "Frederick Douglass proposes to publish in Cleveland, Ohio, a WEEKLY ANTI-SLAVERY PAPER, with the above title."

9 *North Star*, December 3, 1847.

Douglass urged his listeners to subscribe."[10] Such efforts brought him down to New York City and eventually to Brooklyn.

On April 16, 1849, Douglass made his first public appearance in Brooklyn, at Reverend James N. Gloucester's Siloam Presbyterian Church on Myrtle Avenue at the edge of what is now Downtown Brooklyn. According to the *Ram's Horn*'s report (which Douglass reprinted in his paper), the speaker had a dual purpose: "to lecture us on the subject of improvement, and [to] procure subscribers for the *North Star*." In his own account, Douglass observed that Siloam's location at that time was a "beautiful and commodious church under the pastoral care of Mr. Gloucester"; he also noted that after his talk, Van Rensselaer (with whom he stayed) made a "warm and vigorous appeal for the *North Star*."[11] Both reports commended Reverend Gloucester and his Manhattan counterpart, Reverend Pennington, for allowing Douglass to use their churches without charging admission, which stood in contrast to Zion AME in lower Manhattan. Like Pennington, Gloucester remained a prominent figure in New York abolitionism. In February 1858, he and his wife Elizabeth, a savvy businesswoman who helped finance the construction of

10 William S. McFeely, *Frederick Douglass* (New York: W.W. Norton & Co., 1991), 155.
11 *North Star,* May 4, 1849.

Siloam's first full church, would host John Brown for a week at their home in Downtown Brooklyn.[12]

The black community's attempts to build its future in the fast-growing city would be chronicled first in the pages of the *North Star*, where Douglass regularly printed letters from correspondents based elsewhere. Joseph C. Holly, a shoemaker by trade, was the paper's man in Brooklyn. In a May 1849 dispatch, Holly reported about an abolitionist gathering at which the mention of Douglass's name brought forth a "most rapturous applause."[13] That July, Father Theobald Mathew, a leading temperance advocate from Ireland, made a high-profile visit to Brooklyn. As Holly noted in the *North Star*, Mathew, who had met with Douglass in Cork a few years earlier, now "took him by the hand in Brooklyn"—a notable gesture of solidarity in an increasingly hostile racial climate.[14] In 1851, the annual May meeting of the American Anti-Slavery Society had

12 According to the church's website, in 1849 Siloam was located on Myrtle, then in 1850 moved to Prince Street between Myrtle and Willoughby (near Long Island University); it is now on Jefferson Avenue in Bedford-Stuyvesant. Elizabeth Gloucester first made money in retail clothing and later ran a boardinghouse in Brooklyn Heights. As Brooklyn expanded in the 1860s, she bought several lots of real estate in Park Slope and elsewhere, and by the time of her death in 1883, she was reportedly the richest black woman in the US. James Gloucester's father was the first ordained black Presbyterian minister in Philadelphia. He had known Douglass since at least 1843, when the two attended the Colored Convention in Buffalo. For more about the Gloucesters, see Montrose Morris, "Walkabout: The Gloucester Family," *Brownstoner*, October 2012, http://www.brownstoner.com/history/walkabout-the-gloucester-family-of-brooklyn.

13 *North Star*, May 25, 1849.

14 *North Star*, August 31, 1849.

to be moved out of Manhattan because of increasing antiabolitionist violence, and organizers quickly found that they were not welcome in Brooklyn, either. (The gathering took place in Syracuse.) That summer, the *North Star* became *Frederick Douglass' Paper*, which brought the editor closer to Gerrit Smith (who bankrolled the publication), a move that caused a hostile split between Douglass and Garrison.[15]

In the pages of *Frederick Douglass' Paper*, Brooklyn correspondents assumed a more prominent role. In April 1852, James N. Still, a self-employed tailor who used the pen name "Observer," highlighted the success of a recent series of talks in Brooklyn by Reverend Pennington as well as Beecher's growing prominence in local abolitionist circles. In Still's view, such efforts suggested that the "time will come" soon when Douglass would join that network of speakers in the area. Though Brooklyn was announced on his tour itinerary in early 1855, the event never happened, and Douglass's first widely publicized lecture would not take place in the city until 1859.[16] Yet as recorded by his paper's most

---

15 Garrison rejected politics, insisting instead upon "moral suasion" as abolitionists' best course of action, whereas Smith was a key player in the antislavery Liberty Party. As he joined forces with Smith, Douglass also no longer espoused Garrison's view that the Constitution was a "pro-slavery" document. See McFeely, *Frederick Douglass*, 167–171.

16 *Frederick Douglass' Paper*, April 1, 1852. In January 1855, Douglass announced in his paper that he would be giving a lecture—on the history of the "Anti-Slavery Movement"—in Manhattan on January 25 and Brooklyn on January 26. However, in the January 26 issue, the *Paper* reported that earlier that week, Beecher had

prolific Brooklyn correspondent, William "Ethiop" Wilson, Douglass made well-received visits to Brooklyn in the middle of the decade. Included in the more than fifty letters that the editor would publish from Ethiop, a school principal in Weeksville, was mention of Douglass's February 1855 visit to Plymouth Church. He attended with Lewis Tappan, now a member of Beecher's congregation, and the two sat together in Tappan's centrally located pew. According to Ethiop, Douglass was "the observed of all observers, and the lion of the occasion," disrupting the "pious devotions" of the church service. Beecher's name had shown up frequently, and favorably, in Douglass's publications for the preceding seven years, and the editor also mentioned that he had visited Plymouth at least one other time, in May 1854.[17]

Throughout the 1850s, Beecher ascended to prominence as an abolitionist, and the theatrical performer became a fixture on the national lecture circuit. At the same time, the *Independent* also enabled him to reach audiences beyond those who came to Plymouth Church. Launched in late 1848 as both a Congregationalist and abolitionist publication, the weekly paper's driving force in the next decade was publisher Henry C. Bowen, a Brooklyn resident, Lewis Tappan's son-in-law, and a successful merchant who had helped found Plymouth

---

urged his congregation to attend Douglass's lecture at the Broadway Tabernacle in Manhattan, suggesting that the two dates had been combined into one.

17 *Frederick Douglass' Paper*, May 19, 1854, and February 9, 1855.

Church. Yet as Beecher's fame grew, the *Independent* came to be seen as his vehicle. In 1857, Bowen, realizing that the freewheeling minister needed some help managing the publication, hired a brash twenty-two-year-old New York City journalist named Theodore Tilton.[18] Toward the decade's end, Tilton established his national reputation as an abolitionist when the *Independent* published his widely reprinted interview with Mary Brown on the eve of her husband John's execution. (On her way to and from Harpers Ferry, Mary stayed at Tilton's home in Brooklyn.) As the Civil War began, the *Independent* was a leading national voice of abolition, with regular contributions from Horace Greeley, poet John Greenleaf Whittier, and its figurehead's sister, Harriet Beecher Stowe. At the behest of Tilton, who steered the ship in the 1860s, Douglass soon joined those ranks.

In the several years prior to his January 1859 lecture in Williamsburgh, Douglass did not make any noteworthy public appearances in Brooklyn. But during that time he served as a lightning rod for the virulently proslavery *Brooklyn Eagle*. In August 1855, the paper warned of "Fred Douglass, the Negro co-laborer of the white-skin[n]ed niggers of Abolition . . . The doctrines of this fellow are that slaves should not only run away but murder their employers before starting." In 1857,

---

18 For the early history of the *Independent*, see Debby Applegate, *The Most Famous Man in America: The Biography of Henry Ward Beecher* (New York: Doubleday, 2006), 289–291.

the Supreme Court sanctioned such hostilities, issuing its landmark *Dred Scott* decision declaring that slaves were property rather than people. When Dred Scott, the person in question, died in September 1858, the *Eagle* compared him to leading black public figures. Most absurdly, the paper declared that "Fred Douglass, the smartest darkey we have produced, will leave no name beyond his generation, but Dred Scott, a poor simple-minded old Negro . . . will live in the annals of this great nation, as connected with a great constitutional principle."[19] Such blatant racism in the daily local papers no doubt fueled the resolve of John Brown's supporters, and during 1858 and 1859, the Gloucesters actively participated in planning for the Harpers Ferry raid. Douglass, in turn, worked closely with the Brooklyn couple in aiding Brown. In February 1858, Brown left Douglass's home in Rochester and one of his next stops was the Gloucesters' place at 265 Bridge Street (now MetroTech) for the aforementioned weeklong stay. As noted by the pioneering black historian Benjamin Quarles, there Brown informed his Brooklyn hosts that any money sent on his behalf should be directed to Douglass in Rochester. In welcoming Brown to their home, James Gloucester told him, "I wish you Godspeed in your glorious work."[20]

---

19 *Brooklyn Daily Eagle*, August 29, 1856, and September 22, 1858.

20 Benjamin Quarles, *Allies for Freedom: Blacks and John Brown* (New York: Oxford University Press, 1974), 39–41. Gloucester's February 19, 1858, letter to

Douglass, the Gloucesters, and an array of familiar New York City–area names would soon appear regularly in the pages of the *Weekly Anglo-African*, a publication that debuted in July 1859 (as an offshoot of an eponymous magazine). The publishers were two African American brothers from Brooklyn, Thomas and Robert Hamilton,[21] while its eventual leading editor was Douglass's friend James McCune Smith,[22] who moved to Williamsburgh after the Draft Riots of 1863. Along with Douglass and Smith, the *Anglo-African*'s roster of regular contributors included New York City ministers Pennington and Henry Highland Garnet, Douglass's longtime editorial companions Martin Delany and William C. Nell, and Brooklyn mainstays Reverend Gloucester, William J. Wilson, and Junius C. Morel. Despite such an all-star cast (and modest financial backing from Gerrit Smith), the paper struggled financially, and two years after its founding, the Hamiltons temporarily ceded control to James Redpath, a leading white proponent of Haiti colonization schemes for freed slaves (which Douglass briefly supported). In the summer of 1861, James McCune Smith, an opponent of colonization,

---

Brown with the "Godspeed" statement is on p. 4.

21 Copies of the paper were sold at a dress shop run by Hamilton family members on Navy Street near Siloam Church. According to a classified ad in the *Anglo-African*, Hamilton lived nearby at 54 Talman Street (later wiped out by the Brooklyn-Queens Expressway).

22 A prominent black doctor and author, Smith wrote the introduction to *My Bondage and My Freedom* (1855), Douglass's second autobiography.

led a successful effort to restore the Hamiltons' control of the publication.[23] Over the ensuing several issues, a fundraising letter from James Gloucester appeared atop the *Anglo-African*'s editorial page. That November, the paper began serializing Martin Delany's novel *Blake; or the Huts of America*—and early the next year, the author, a leading early voice of pan-Africanism, listed his address as 97 High Street, at the edge of Brooklyn Heights.[24] Like the *Independent*, the *Anglo-African*'s office was in Manhattan (near Park Row), but it was closely identified with Brooklyn.

The *Anglo-African* also provided extensive coverage of the assault on Harpers Ferry, including important details regarding Douglass's role in supporting John Brown, a matter of historical dispute.[25] In mid-August 1859, Douglass stayed overnight at the Gloucesters' home on his way to meet Brown in Chambersburg, Pennsylvania; while in town, the *Anglo-African* noted at the time, Douglass stopped by their office for "a short visit." A few weeks later, the paper reported that

---

23 See John R. McKivigan's biography of Redpath, *Forgotten Firebrand* (Ithaca, NY: Cornell University Press, 2008), 73. Redpath was a strong supporter of John Brown.

24 *Weekly Anglo-African*, January 4, 1862.

25 Douglass and Brown had been close allies for more than a decade. Most accounts suggest that Douglass had a change of heart at the Chambersburg meeting with Brown in late August 1859. But well into the twentieth century, Brown's descendants believed that Douglass had pledged to join the assault on Harpers Ferry. See Louis A. DeCaro, *John Brown: The Cost of Freedom* (New York: International Publishers, 2007), 63–69.

"Frederick Douglass, Esq., will leave this city [New York] in early November, on a lecturing tour through Great Britain."[26] It was a seemingly uncontroversial announcement, but Douglass would later use his stated travel plans as evidence that he was not planning to join Brown in Virginia, a charge leveled against him at the time. Like the leading daily papers in New York and Brooklyn, the *Anglo-African* documented the mid-October attack and its aftermath in exhaustive detail. Meanwhile, proslavery forces—led by the *New York Herald*—eagerly sought to implicate Douglass, who at the end of October fired back at his accusers in a letter to the *Rochester Democrat*. Though he did not denounce Brown and company, Douglass denied that he had "encouraged" their actions. He further insisted that he would never make any "promise so rash and wild" as a vow to participate.[27]

Over the course of three issues in late October and early November, the *Anglo-African* published a lengthy chronicle of Brown's weeklong trial. Compiled from various newspaper accounts, the series' final installment closed with a sampling of the material found in Brown's carpetbag after his capture. Of the 102 letters in Brown's possession, the paper printed two. The first read:

---

26 *Weekly Anglo-African*, September 10, 1859.
27 Douglass's letter was reprinted in the *Weekly Anglo-African*, November 11, 1859.

Brooklyn August 18 '59

Esteemed Friend

*I gladly avail myself of the opportunity of-
fered by our friend Mr. F. Douglass, who has
just called upon us previous to his visit to you,
to enclose to you for the good cause in which
you are such a zealous laborer. A small amount
[ten dollars] which please accept with my most
ardent wishes for its, and your, benefit.*

*The visit of our mutual Friend Douglass has
somewhat revived my rather drooping spirits
in the cause, but seeing such ambition & enterprise in him I am again encouraged. [W]ith
best wishes for your welfare and prosperity &
the good of your Cause. I subscribe myself Your
sincere friend*

MRS. E.A. GLOUCESTER
Please write to me with best respects to your son.

In the second letter, James H. Harris, a black
friend of Brown's in Cleveland, mentioned the trouble
he was having raising funds there, complaining of the
lack of resolve of the "whole Negro set."[28] While the
Anglo-African's selections seem intended to illustrate

---

28 *Ibid.*

the sturdy support for Brown received from his closest black allies in Brooklyn—the Gloucesters—Elizabeth's communique also clearly identified Douglass's role as a conduit of material support. The latter's own dispatch to the *Rochester Democrat*, in which he denied any role in Brown's actions, followed the letters from Gloucester and Harris. Although the excerpts ran without introductory comment, the many members of Douglass's inner circle who read the *Anglo-African* no doubt knew the score: Douglass was clearly implicated in Brown's assault on slavery.

In the aftermath of the Civil War, John Brown would serve as one key touchstone for Douglass, and Abraham Lincoln would be another. Douglass did not meet Lincoln until August 1863, but the two had common friends and associates. In late February 1860, Lincoln came to see Beecher in action at Plymouth Church, the initial planned location for the landmark antislavery speech he ended up delivering the next day at Cooper Union; the *Independent*'s Bowen and Tilton served as coorganizers of the Great Hall event.[29] When Douglass began to make high-profile appearances in Brooklyn in February 1863, Lincoln became a central figure in his lectures. Though Douglass came to like the president

29 See Harold Holzer, *Lincoln and the Power of the Press* (New York: Simon & Schuster, 2014), 216–220. Holzer argues that Lincoln paraphrased Douglass in the concluding line of his speech.

personally, he was often frustrated with Lincoln's cautious handling of the war. But as historian Eric Foner observes, in the aftermath of the president's assassination, Douglass began to elevate the fallen leader's heroism, praising Lincoln in order "to get people's support for Reconstruction."[30] Such calculations were evident in many of Douglass's Brooklyn appearances, most poignantly during his rousing January 1866 speech at the Brooklyn Academy of Music (BAM), when he sang Lincoln's praises and relentlessly trashed Andrew Johnson.

At that same BAM event, Douglass denounced the upsurge in anti–black equality sentiment stirring in Brooklyn, which the speaker had encountered firsthand during the run-up to the lecture. As he became close allies with Tilton, Douglass now experienced some ups and downs with Beecher—and after those two figures had their famous blowup in the 1870s, Douglass remained in Tilton's camp.[31] In the speeches Douglass gave in Brooklyn during the Civil War and Reconstruction, the stars of John Brown and Abe Lincoln shone brightly. It was fitting, then, that the last two major ad-

---

30 "Struggle and Progress," an interview with Eric Foner, *Jacobin*, Summer 2015.
31 Tilton became a leading national journalist during the 1860s, thus taking him on the road. While he was away, Beecher spent lots of time at the Tiltons' Brooklyn home (174 Livingston Street), where he and Elizabeth Tilton had an affair. In 1872, Victoria Woodhull—like Theodore, a proponent of "free love"—helped expose the scandal; Douglass was nominated as Woodhull's vice-presidential candidate that year. Theodore Tilton was effectively run out of Brooklyn a few years later, and spent the last three decades of his life in Paris. See Applegate, *The Most Famous Man in America.*

dresses Douglass delivered in Brooklyn focused on the lives of these two pivotal figures.

Whether at BAM, Plymouth Church, or Bridge Street AME, at an Emancipation Jubilee in Bedford-Stuyvesant or the Union League in Crown Heights, Douglass struck up lively conversations with his audiences. During the Civil War and into Reconstruction, he also continued to incur heavy fire from the *Brooklyn Eagle*. In the following selections of his speeches and responses to them,[32] we see Douglass's brilliance on display, and in the process learn a bit about the Brooklyn he knew well.

Editor's Note

In editing the speeches, my goal was to present as accurately as possible what Douglass stated at each of the

---

32 Douglass made three other notable appearances not included in this collection. In May 1863, he attended a meeting of the African Civilization Society in Weeksville. Along with Henry Highland Garnet, two of Douglass's longtime colleagues, Martin Delany and Junius C. Morel, were promoting a black-led colonization effort in Liberia. At the gathering, Douglass spoke briefly but forcefully against colonization, arguing that America was the "place black men were to develop and become great." See Judith Wellman, *Brooklyn's Promised Land* (New York University Press, 2014), Chap. 3.

In 1869, Douglass made two more appearances at BAM. The first, in mid-January, was a lecture on William the Silent (a.k.a. William of Orange), the sixteenth-century Dutch figurehead. The subject was one of Douglass's more scholarly pursuits. In May, he participated in a far more topical discussion, at a meeting of the American Equal Rights Association, the suffragist group. Though he was a resolute proponent of women's right to vote, Douglass at the time argued stridently against Susan B. Anthony and Elizabeth Cady Stanton's opposition to the Fifteenth Amendment (on the grounds that it excluded women). However, there's little record of what Douglass actually said at the Brooklyn event, at which Beecher and Lucretia Mott also spoke.

Brooklyn events. Some of the lectures here (Chapters 1, 3, and 8) combine Douglass's published versions with accounts from newspapers. Others rely primarily on newspaper transcriptions of the speeches (Chapters 2, 4–7, and 9). At the end of the brief introductions to each chapter, I identify the main sources.

So as not to distract readers by noting every typo or unclear pronoun found in the newspaper coverage, I simply fixed some of them. Similarly, in certain portions of the speeches, I adhered to contemporary rules for capitalization (especially regarding proper nouns) and modernized some punctuation (particularly in the use of dashes). Rather than insert repeated or unclear ellipses, I chose to summarize in parentheses (or footnotes) the gist of any substantial deletions. For ease of readability, I inserted occasional paragraph returns. In general, most of the inconsistencies—in spelling, punctuation, and grammar—from the original texts of both the speeches and the newspaper reports have nonetheless been retained. The small changes noted above were made solely for the sake of clarity to the reader.

—*T.H.*

CHAPTER I

SELF-MADE MEN

Williamsburgh, with Walt Whitman
January 1859

Douglass's first widely promoted appearance in Brooklyn occurred in early January of 1859. Williamsburgh, home to an established black community, had only become part of Brooklyn in 1855. Accordingly, the *Williamsburgh Times* (founded in 1848) became the *Brooklyn Daily Times,* and from 1857–1859 the paper's editor was Walt Whitman.

According to biographer David S. Reynolds, Whitman grew increasingly conservative on racial issues during the period just before the Civil War, at one point asking rhetorically in a *Daily Times* editorial, "Is not America for the Whites? And is it not better so?" A supporter neither of slavery nor of black equality, Whitman—like many of his contemporaries, including Lincoln—at the time advocated colonization.[33] Even so, he continued to hold Douglass in high esteem.

---

33 David S. Reynolds, *Walt Whitman's America: A Cultural Biography* (New York: Knopf, 1995), 372–373.

Douglass came to Brooklyn to present, for only the second time, what would become a stock speech in his repertoire, on "Self-Made Men."[34] He gave the lecture at the Odeon, a theater on 5th Street (now Driggs Avenue) between S. 3rd and S. 4th Streets. Due to inclement weather, attendance was sparse. But Whitman was in the audience. Here is his account in the *Daily Times*, followed by a sampling of Douglass's speech.

※

Brooklyn Daily Times

SATURDAY EVENING, JANUARY 8, 1859

"FRED. DOUGLASS' LECTURE"

The lecture of this gentleman, which was delivered at the Odeon last evening, pursuant to announcement, was quite slimly attended, the unfavorable state of the weather having kept many persons at home who would otherwise have been present.

Mr. Douglass was very much confined to his notes, and was not so fluent as we remember him to have been some years ago.[35] He has a splendid voice, loud, clear

---

34 Douglass debuted the speech one day earlier at Reverend James W.C. Pennington's Shiloh Presbyterian Church in Manhattan. He would give the talk more than fifty times before his death in 1895. See *The Frederick Douglass Papers*, Series 1, Vol. 5, John W. Blassingame and John R. McKivigan, eds. (New Haven, CT: Yale University Press, 1992), 535.

35 According to Reynolds (p. 121), Whitman attended a speech by Douglass at

and sonorous, which would make itself heard in the largest open-air assembly. His lecture was upon "Self-Made Men"—rather a trite topic, but quite appropriate when the antecedents of the lecturer are considered. He was liberally applauded at various points of his discourse, where he alluded to his past history, or spoke of the circumstances under which he had himself risen to a prominent position.

He commenced by alluding to the many illustrious examples of self-made men in all ages, and the causes that had given them prominence. The celebrated Negro, Touissant L'Ouverture, was mentioned first, together with several other colored men who had achieved greatness—the lecturer apologizing for mentioning them first, as his past experience had been chiefly among "that class of people." [Horace] Greeley, of the *Tribune*, was mentioned next as evidence of what self-denying industry and unflagging perseverance can accomplish when directed into worthy channels.

Putting aside the blot of slavery, the lecturer looked upon America as the natural home of self-made men. In no country in the world were the conditions under which such men are trained more favorable than in America. Here these men were found in high places. They were represented among our senators, savants, poets and historians.

---

the August 1848 Free Soil Party convention in Buffalo.

This was the gist of the lecture, which we must be excused from reporting at length. The various antislavery allusions with which Mr. Douglass interspersed his discourse and which he lost no opportunity of introducing, appeared to be warmly relished by the audience.

Excerpt from "Self-Made Men"[36]

Mr. [Ralph Waldo] Emerson has declared that it is natural to believe in great men. Whether this is a fact, or not, we do believe in them and worship them. The Visible God of the New Testament is revealed to us as a man of like passions with ourselves. We seek out our wisest and best man, the man who, by eloquence or the sword compels us to believe him such, and make him our leader, prophet, preacher and lawgiver. We do this not because he is essentially different from us, but because of his identity with us. He is our best representative and reflects, on a colossal scale, the scale to which we would aspire, our highest aims, objects, powers and possibilities.

This natural reverence for all that is great in man, and this tendency to deify and worship him, though natural and the source of man's elevation, has not always shown itself wise but has often shown itself far otherwise than wise. It has often given us a wicked ruler for a righteous one, a false prophet for a true one, a corrupt

---

36 This version of the speech is from 1872.

preacher for a pure one, a man of war for a man of peace, and a distorted and vengeful image of God for an image of justice and mercy.

But it is not my purpose to attempt here any comprehensive and exhaustive theory or philosophy or the nature of manhood in all the range I have indicated. I am here to speak to you of a peculiar type of manhood under the title of "*Self-Made Men.*"

That there is, in more respects than one, something like a solecism in this title, I freely admit. Properly speaking, there are in the world no such men as self-made men. That term implies an individual independence of the past and present which can never exist.

Our best and most valued acquisitions have been obtained either from our contemporaries or from those who have preceded us in the field of thought and discovery. We have all either begged, borrowed or stolen. We have reaped where others have sown, and that which others have strown, we have gathered. It must in truth be said, though it may not accord well with self-conscious individuality and self-conceit, that no possible native force of character, and no depth of wealth and originality, can lift a man into absolute independence of his fellowmen, and no generation of men can be independent of the preceding generation. The brotherhood and inter-dependence of mankind are guarded and defended at all points. I believe in individuality, but individuals are, to the mass, like waves to the ocean. The highest order of genius is as dependent as is the lowest. It, like the loftiest waves of the sea, derives its power and greatness from the grandeur and vastness of the ocean of which it forms a part. We differ as the waves, but are one as the sea.

Self-made men are the men who, under peculiar difficulties and without the ordinary helps of favoring circumstances, have attained knowledge, usefulness, power and position and have learned from themselves the best uses to which life can be put in this world, and in the exercises of these uses to build up worthy character. They are the men who owe little or nothing to birth, relationship, friendly surroundings; to wealth inherited or to early approved means of education; who are what they are, without the aid of any favoring conditions by which other men usually rise in the world and achieve great results. In fact they are the men who are not brought up but who are obliged to come up, not only without the voluntary assistance or friendly co-operation of society, but often in open and derisive defiance of all the efforts of society and the tendency of circumstances to repress, retard and keep them down. They are the men who, in a world of schools, academies, colleges and other institutions of learning, are often compelled by unfriendly circumstances to acquire their education elsewhere and, amidst unfavorable conditions, to hew out for themselves a way to success, and thus to become the architects of their own good fortunes.

They are in a peculiar sense indebted to themselves for themselves. If they have traveled far, they have made the road on which they have traveled. If they have ascended high, they have built their own ladder. From the depths of poverty [men] such as these have often come. From the heartless pavements of large and crowded cities; barefooted, homeless, and friendless, they have come. From hunger, rags and destitution, they have come; motherless and fatherless, they have come, and may come. Flung overboard in the midnight storm on the broad and tempest-tossed ocean of life—left without ropes, planks, oars or life-preservers—they have bravely buffeted the frowning billows and have risen in safety and life where others, supplied with the best appliances for safety and success, have fainted, despaired and gone down forever.

Such men as these, whether found in one position or another, whether in the college or in the factory; whether professors or plowmen; whether Caucasian or Indian; whether Anglo-Saxon or Anglo-African, are self-made men and are entitled to a certain measure of respect for their success and for proving to the world the grandest possibilities of human nature, of whatever variety of race or color.

Among my dark examples I can name no man with more satisfaction than I can Toussaint L'Ouverture, the hero of Santo Domingo. [B]orn a slave and held a slave till he was fifteen years of age, like [Benjamin] Banneker,[37] he was black and showed no trace of Caucasian admixture. [H]istory hands him down to us as a brave and generous soldier, a wise and powerful statesman, an ardent patriot and a successful liberator of his people and his country.

The contemporaries of this Haitian chief paint him as without a single moral blemish; while friends and foes alike, accord him the highest ability. In his eulogies no modern hero has been more fortunate than Toussaint L'Ouverture. History, poetry and eloquence have vied with each other to do him reverence. Wordsworth and [John Greenleaf] Whittier have, in characteristic verse, encircled his brow with a halo of fadeless glory.[38] The testimony of these and a thousand others who have come up from depths of society, confirms the theory that industry is the most potent factor in the success of self-made men, and thus raises the dignity of labor; for whatever may be one's natural gifts, success, as I have said, is due mainly to this great means, open and free to all.

While the world values skill and power, it values beauty and polish as well. It was not alone the hard good sense and honest heart of Horace Greeley, the self-made man, that made the *New York Tribune*, but like-

---

37 Pioneering eighteenth-century astronomer and author born to a free black mother and freed slave father.

38 Wordsworth composed a sonnet titled "To Toussaint L'Ouverture" in 1802; Whittier, a Quaker poet and abolitionist (whose work appeared frequently in the *Independent*), penned a lengthy ode in 1833.

wise the brilliant and thoroughly educated men silently associated with him.

There never was a self-made man, however well-educated, who, with the same exertion, would not have been better educated by the aid of schools and colleges. The charge is made and well sustained, that self-made men are not generally over-modest or self-forgetful men. It was said of Horace Greeley that he was a self-made man and worshipped his maker. Perhaps the strong resistance which such men meet in maintaining their claim, may account for much of their self-assertion.

CHAPTER 2

THE BLACK MAN AND THE WAR

Bridge Street AME
February 1863

I n the winter of 1863, Douglass sought to build on the momentum generated by the Emancipation Proclamation, which Lincoln formally issued on January 1. In addition to freeing slaves in Confederate states, the Proclamation also encouraged black participation in the war effort. Douglass became a leading voice in support of enlistment—but stressed that black soldiers should simultaneously acquire full rights of citizenship.

On February 7, Douglass gave a well-received version of the following speech at Cooper Union—with both Robert Hamilton of the *Anglo-African* and Theodore Tilton of the *Independent* joining him onstage.[39] Twelve days later, Douglass came to Brooklyn at the invitation of

---

39 As noted by Sydney Howard Gay of the *New York Tribune*, at the end of Douglass's talk, Hamilton sang the "new John Brown song" (see note 45 below) and Tilton explained how local sentiment had grown more favorable to Brown since the war started. See *New York Tribune*, February 7, 1863.

Reverend James Morris Williams,[40] minister of the Bridge Street African Methodist Episcopal Church (Bridge Street AME). Blacks reportedly comprised two-thirds of the approximately four hundred people in attendance.

The *Brooklyn Daily Eagle* incorrectly states that it was Douglass's "first appearance in Brooklyn." More accurately, it was his first widely advertised lecture in the city's central area. At the time, the church was located at 309 Bridge Street in Downtown Brooklyn.[41] During the Civil War, the Democratic *Eagle*—edited by Thomas Kinsella, an Irish immigrant—was no champion of the Union cause.

Note that I have added parentheses and italics to some passages below to distinguish between the newspaper's account and Douglass's speech.

✳

THE BROOKLYN DAILY EAGLE

FEBRUARY 20, 1863

FRED. DOUGLASS IN BROOKLYN   THE BLACK MAN AND THE WAR

Frederick Douglass, the only representative of the col-

---

40 Williams was an active abolitionist who had burned a procolonization tract at the 1855 Colored Convention. See Craig Steven Wilder, *A Covenant with Color: Race and Social Power in Brooklyn* (New York: Columbia University Press, 1999), 174.

41 The original building still exists, but is now the Wunsch Building, located within MetroTech and owned by New York University. In 1938, Bridge Street AME moved to its present location, 277 Stuyvesant Avenue in Bedford-Stuyvesant.

ored people of the United States who has by his natural abilities attained any eminence at home or abroad, made his first appearance in Brooklyn last night at the African Church in Bridge Street, to deliver a lecture on the war. Considering the position of the lecturer, the subject he was to treat of and the fact that the proceeds were to be applied for the benefit of the Church, the colored brethren did not turn out very handsomely, and if the white folks had not come to the rescue, there would not have been a rather slim audience. There were between three and four hundred persons present, of whom about one third were white. Among the latter were a few prominent local politicians of the Republican persuasion.

Fred. Douglass made his appearance at 8 o'clock, in company with the pastor of the church and another brother. Douglass is a bright mulatto, of fine physical proportions, standing nearly six feet in height, and of athletic build. His features are more of the Caucasian than African cast; he has a high, broad forehead, giving him an intellectual expressive countenance. He sports a moustache and goatee, and his hair, which is quite abundant and slightly tinged with grey, as a sort of compromise between the African tendency to curl, and the limpness of the Caucasian capillary, stands out straight in all directions.

As a speaker Douglass will compare favorably with the white abolition actors; his elocution is very fine, his language clear and forcible, while he discusses the slavery question in a far more rational manner than most of his white co-laborers in the cause. He spoke last evening for two hours and enchained the attention of his auditors. The subject of his lecture was "The Black Man and the War." He said:—

We are here as Abolitionists—as colored Abolitionists—and as citizens of the United States; but more especially as men, having the interest of the whole human family at heart. Desiring that this nation, which is our common inheritance, may be preserved in all its integrity and completeness. Viewing this great issue not from the narrow standpoint of Abolitionists, but regarding it in its relation to the whole world, [t]he question [be]comes how shall the land be preserved? How can the institutions of the United States be preserved?

([Douglass] believed that the only hope of the government lay in coupling its interests with the interests of the four millions of slaves. He could give many reasons for this.)

This Union can never be re-established on the old basis of compromise. If we of the North were disposed to make concessions, the slave-holders of the South would reject any propositions of the kinds . . . In order to live together peaceably the North and the South must have something in common between them.

(The speaker then went on to argue the irreconcilability of the institution of slavery with the freedom of the North.)

Slavery must be paramount over all other interests of state, church, social and family relations—more sacred than all else is slavery at the South. The North has hitherto conceded everything the South has asked; has always been conciliating, trying to make the South love us.

([Douglass] instanced the concessions made to slavery from the admission of Texas, to the Fugitive Slave law, and the repeal of the Missouri Compromise.)

Was the South satisfied with this? No! They said we must vote for the man they chose for President, but thank God, one million eight hundred thousand voters rolled our long and able Abe Lincoln into the chair. [*Applause.*]

(The speaker then proceeded to answer the question what will the black man do, and said:)

We will stand by the president with our sympathies, black though we are; we will stand by him with our strong arms, black though we are [*applause*], provided the same rights are guaranteed to us as to men who come this land, who have no such claim as we have. We have watered your soil with our tears, enriched it with our sweat, tilled it with our labor, and we ask the same privileges as men who come from abroad—who are not born here. But it is said that the Proclamation is a violation of the Constitution of the United States. In regard to this [I] would say that the Constitution of the United States, important though it may be, was in no respect so important as the people of the United

States, who made it. The hat a man wears should never be made more sacred than his head. The hat is made for the head, not the head for the hat. The Constitution of the United States was made by and for the people of the United States.

([Douglass] conceded that it was an evidence of the great wisdom of the fathers of the Republic, but he believed that the people of the present generation could make a constitution just as good as the old constitution, should they put their wits together for the purpose. Nevertheless, he did not consider there had been any violation of the Constitution, but it was a convenient argument for the Copperheads to use.[42])

They say the Constitution provides that a man should not be deprived of his property, or his liberty, without process of law . . . Does the Constitution grant any right to property in man? On the contrary its provisions guarantee liberty to every slave in the United States. Men of narrow views, who cater to the prejudices of the multitude, say this is a white man's government. Some time ago a party sprung up here which claimed that native-born Americans only, constituted the nationality. This nation was made up of all nationalities. Every race in existence had representatives here; the Constitution of the United States recognizes the whole, and provides for the whole. It does not say, "We the

---

42 Copperheads were the most openly proslavery Northern faction of the Democrats.

people of Anglo-Saxon descent, we the people of Celtic descent, we the Germans, we the French." What does it say? "We, the people" do ordain to establish this government. For what? To provide for the common defense and general welfare; to establish justice, to secure the blessings of peace for ourselves and families. In eleven out of thirteen states which adopted that constitution the black man was a legal voter. The first blood shed in the defense of the liberties of this country was that of a black man in the city of Boston. Look in the Constitution: there is not a word about the white man, or the black man; not a word about slaves or masters. No, slavery had no guarantee in the Constitution, and as it has snatched up the sword, let it perish by the sword.[43]

(The speaker regarded the Proclamation as the great event of the 19th century. [It was] important not only to his people, but to the government itself, which needed it in the prosecution of the war, because it needed to place itself in a position to deserve success.)

It is said of us, and with propriety, in Europe, as well as at home, that while the South is fighting for slavery, we are not fighting against it. The Proclamation will do

---

43 In the 1840s, Douglass strongly adhered to an opposite interpretation, most closely associated with his then-ally William Lloyd Garrison. Garrison insisted that the Constitution was a "pro-slavery" document; as evidence, he cited both the Three-Fifths Clause and the Fugitive Slave Clause. Douglass broke with Garrison in the early 1850s, and began espousing the position stated here. Technically, Douglass's point is correct: the words *slave* and *slavery* appeared in neither of those two clauses, nor did they show up anywhere else in the Constitution. But the intent of those two key provisions was clear when the Constitution was written.

more for the Union than a thousand such victories as we have won during the past two years. It is producing its effect on the other side of the Atlantic. There is not a potentate in Europe who rules by "divine right" but sympathizes with the men who are trying to break up this government. We need this Proclamation to arouse the democratic masses who will stand between us and the aristocracy of England and the machinations of Napoleon, who is already evincing a design to interfere on behalf of the South.[44]

The people want to know how colored men feel, what they think and what they will do. We feel good. [*Laughter*.] We are jubilant just now. We wake up in the night singing "John Brown's body lies moldering in his grave."[45]

Sing it first thing in the morning and the last thing at night. We have learned to pronounce the name of Lincoln, though some will persist in calling it "Linkum." [*Laughter*.] We feel good; we now see where you stand and where we stand.

(The speaker said he had predicted at the outset of the war this result.)

The North had made the mistake of supposing that

<hr/>

44 Jefferson Davis believed that owing to their reliance of their economies on Southern cotton, both Great Britain and France (ruled by Louis Napoleon Bonaparte) would recognize the Confederacy. Despite overtures like the ones mentioned here, such an alliance never happened.

45 The lyrics to "John Brown's Body" were written by poet Julia Ward Howe and set to the tune of "Battle Hymn of the Republic."

the rebellion could be crushed without interfering with slavery. Nearly all our generals thought so; the only man who saw this error was Fremont.[46] [*Great applause.*] Gen. Butler has been converted to the right doctrine, and now says that the only way to destroy the rebellion is to destroy slavery.[47] They have begun to recruit at the North when they should have been recruiting at the South. There are four million of his people at the South, capable of furnishing eight hundred thousand able-bodied men; and if they were not enough, the women would fight also. The king of Dahomey was kept on his throne by an army of black women. And if our black women cannot shoulder musket, they can do what white soldiers have had to do, and have lost their lives in doing, dig trenches. We must urge the government to be bold; to be as true to the Union and as bold in maintaining it, as the rebels were to their cause. In opening recruiting offices to enlist colored men, the states of Maryland, Kentucky, Missouri, Delaware, Western Virginia, and Tennessee had been excluded. These states

---

46 John C. Fremont was the first presidential candidate of the antislavery Republican Party in 1856 (with his campaign headquarters in Staten Island). Early in the Civil War, Lincoln named him Commander of the Western Armies, but Fremont angered the president by issuing an edict emancipating all slaves in Missouri (prompting Lincoln to relieve him of his command). Douglass and his allies would support Fremont's short-lived presidential candidacy in 1864, in an attempt to pressure Lincoln to fight for full equality.

47 As commander of Fort Monroe in Virginia in 1861, General Benjamin Butler declared fugitive slaves to be contraband of war, thus negating the Fugitive Slave Act.

contained a free colored population of ninety thousand, capable of furnishing fifteen thousand soldiers. Just where we have the power to recruit, we will not open recruiting offices.

[I believe] the Negroes will fight. Those who said they would not were inconsistent in their charges. One day an article would appear in their papers alleging that the Negroes would not fight; the next day they would write an article asserting that the first fruits of the Proclamation would be setting the Negroes to cut their masters' throats. One day they will say that the Negroes will not work; the next they will state that the Negroes are coming north to take the work out the hands of the Germans and Irish. [*Laughter.*] The Negroes will fight when they have something to fight for. They are sensible men, and not anxious to fight unless they have a chance of whipping somebody. The rebel armies have been against them, and the Northern armies have been pledged against them. The Southerners know that the Negroes will fight, hence the watch they keep upon them, and they are always going armed with bowie knife and revolver.

([Douglass] instanced St. Domingo, where France sent an army of twenty thousand men to reduce to slavery men who had for six years enjoyed their liberty.)

The black men drove back the invaders, and have maintained their freedom for sixty years.[48]

---

48 Like many of his contemporaries, Douglass referred to Saint-Domingue as Santo Domingo. Toussaint L'Ouverture and company had forced the French to

(He cited the Amistad slave mutiny and others, where black men have done deeds of bravery, showing they will fight when they have the opportunity of fighting for liberty.[49])

The American Negroes are now willing to fight in this war, provided they have the shield of this government extended over them, and the same rights and protection guaranteed to them as to other men who fight its battles. Their lives are as precious as those of other men, and they have as much regard for their lives as other men. If this protection is guaranteed to the colored men, they will at the North and at the South rally around the flag.

("Give them a chance," was all he asked. If they do not embrace it, then let the colored people forever hold their peace. If it was needed that he, the speaker, should go forth, and he should refuse, then let condemnation settle on his brow, in common with the rest. The speaker continued to discuss the prospects of the war, and expressed his belief that the rebellion would eventually be put down, since the right means [the Emancipation Proclamation] had been adopted.)

❈

abolish slavery in the colony in 1794. In 1801, Napoleon sent in his forces in an attempt to reinstate slavery. The revolutionaries prevailed, turning Saint-Domingue into Haiti in 1804.

49 Douglass is referring to a slave revolt in 1839 aboard a Spanish ship that resulted in an 1841 ruling by the US Supreme Court affirming the freedom of the African captives.

Brooklyn Daily Times

FEBRUARY 20, 1863

THE BLACK MAN AND THE WAR—Fred. Douglass, the colored orator, delivered a lecture on this subject last night, at the African Methodist Episcopal Church in Bridge Street, Western District.[50] It was an able and genuinely rhetorical lecture, and was listened to by a mixed audience of four hundred persons. After laying down the usual fundamental planks of the Abolition creed, [Douglass] proceeded to apply the black man to the war, and maintained that the colored race would fight whenever they were assured that they should be allowed the privileges of citizenship on the same ground with the Germans or Irish. He promised that the blacks would stand by the president with their sympathy, their strong arms, and their earnest hearts. The lecture was heartily applauded.

---

50 After the 1855 incorporation of Williamsburgh and Bushwick into Brooklyn, that part of the city was called the Eastern District, while the greater Brooklyn Heights and downtown area was considered to be the Western District.

CHAPTER 3

WHAT SHALL BE DONE WITH THE NEGRO?

Brooklyn Academy of Music
May 1863

In May of 1863, Douglass came back to Brooklyn in order to amplify his call for full black equality. He made his case by rebutting popular arguments against black "inferiority"; and he critiqued a number of proposals about what to do with freed slaves, from colonization to segregation. Douglass also questioned why the Irish, who had endured religious oppression in their homeland, had now become "persecutors" of black people in America. Two months later, the Draft Riots would starkly illustrate local Irish racist sentiment.

Earlier that week, Douglass had given the same talk at the American Anti-Slavery Society's annual meeting, held at the Church of the Puritans (near Union Square in Manhattan). But the follow-up event—held on May 15 at the Brooklyn Academy of Music, then located at 176–194 Montague Street in Brooklyn Heights—promised to be a good show. An ad in the *Eagle* announced it as a "Grand Rally," highlighting that "Fred. Douglass, Esq., will lecture" and the very popular Hutchinson Family Singers "will sing their favorite songs."

BAM was indeed filled to capacity that Friday night. Postmaster George Lincoln—a white abolitionist, and then the highest-ranking federal official in Brooklyn— served as master of ceremonies. The *Eagle* reported that Senator Samuel Pomeroy, a Kansas Republican, joined Theodore Tilton on the stage, as did a number of "colored people." Writing in the *New York Tribune,* editor Sydney Howard Gay—a leading figure in the Underground Railroad, and a longtime ally of Douglass— observed that "the beauty and fashion of the City of Churches were largely represented in the audience, with here and there a colored lady or a colored gentleman sitting in the audience, as if to demonstrate the fact set forth by the orator of the evening, 'that friend could sit near friend, as easily as master or mistress could sit near servant.'"[51]

Thomas Kinsella of the *Eagle* assumed a far less respectful tone in his editorial about the event, which appeared alongside the paper's recap. What appears first here is the text of the speech, as reprinted in *Frederick*

51 *New York Tribune*, May 16, 1863. The *Eagle* (also May 16, 1863) stated that "the reporter's table was not even free from the general diversity of color, for two Negroes sat at it each with a notebook busily occupied between applauding the speaker and taking notes." Copies of the *Anglo-African* from that year do not exist, but it seems likely that at least one of the Hamiltons was there.

Douglass' Monthly, interspersed with portions of the *Eagle*'s versions of it. (Note that I have added italics to indicate the *Eagle* portions.) That is followed by Kinsella's splenetic reply. Whether it was Douglass's statements about the Irish or his concluding comments about publicly socializing with white women (or both) that set Kinsella off is not clear.

❂

What Shall Be Done with the Negro?

Ladies and Gentlemen

I think that most of you will agree with me in respect to the surpassing importance of the subject we are here to consider this evening though you may differ from me in other respects. It seems to me that the relation subsisting between the white and colored people of this country, is of all other questions, the great, paramount, imperative and all commanding question for this age and nation to solve. [*Cheers.*]

All the circumstances of the hour plead with an eloquence, equaled by no human tongue, for the immediate solution of this vital problem. 200,000 graves—a distracted and bleeding country pleads for this solution. It cannot be denied, nobody now even attempts to deny, that the question, what shall be done with the Negro, is the one grand cause of the tremendous war now upon us, and likely to continue upon us, until the country is united upon some wise policy concerning it. When the country was at peace and all appeared prosperous, there was something like a plausible argument in favor of leaving things to their own course. No such policy avails now. [Cheers.]

We are encompassed by it on every side and burned with [the question] as by fire, and turn which way we will, it meets us at every point. What will be done with the four or five millions of colored people in the United States? The Copperheads may sneer at the question as a nigger question, and seek to degrade it by miscalling and mispronouncing [the word Negro], but in doing so they only degrade themselves. [Cheers.] They talk about the Union as it was and about the Constitution as it is, and pretend to ignore the great question of the day. Nevertheless the Negro will come out; despite all the dust and smoke thrown in his face, the Negro looms up as the pivot upon which the life or death, the salvation and prosperity, or the rain of the republic depend. [Cheers.]

The term, Negro, is at this hour the most pregnant word in the English language. The destiny of the nation has the Negro for its pivot, and turns upon the question as to what shall be done with him. Peace and war, union and disunion, salvation and ruin, glory and shame all crowd upon our thoughts the moment this vital word is pronounced.

You and I have witnessed many attempts to put this Negro question out of the pale of popular thought and discussion, and have seen the utter vanity of all such attempts. It has baffled all the subtle contrivances of an ease-loving and selfish priesthood, and has constantly refused to be smothered under the soft cushions of a canting and heartless religion. It has mocked and defied the compromising cunning of so-called statesmen, who would have gladly postponed our present troubles beyond our allotted space of life and bequeath them as a legacy of sorrow to our children. But this wisdom of the crafty is confounded and their counsels brought to naught. A divine energy, omniscient and omnipotent, acting through the silent, solemn and all-pervading laws of the universe, irresistible, unalterable and eternal, has ever more forced this mighty question of the Negro upon the attention of the country and the world.

What shall be done with the Negro? meets us not only in the street, in the church, in the senate, and in our state legislatures; but in our diplomatic correspondence with foreign nations, and even on the field of battle, where our brave sons and brothers are striking for liberty and country, or for honored graves.

This question met us before the war; it meets us during the war, and will certainly meet us after the war, unless we shall have the wisdom, the courage, and the nobleness of soul to settle the status of the Negro, on the solid and immovable bases of eternal justice.

I stand here tonight therefore, to advocate what I conceive to be such a solid basis, one that shall fix our peace upon a rock. Putting aside all the hay, wood and stubble of expediency, I shall advocate for the Negro, his most full and complete adoption into the great national family of America. I shall demand for him the most perfect civil and political equality, and that he shall enjoy all the rights, privileges and immunities enjoyed by any other members of the body politic. [*Cheers.*] I weigh my words and I mean all I say, when I contend as I do contend, that this is the *only solid, and* final solution of the problem before us. It is demanded not less by the terrible exigencies of the nation, than by the Negro himself for the Negro and the nation, are to rise or fall, be killed or cured, saved or lost together. Save the Negro and you save the nation, destroy the Negro and you destroy the nation, and to save both you must have but one great law of Liberty, Equality and Fraternity for all Americans without respect to color. [*Cheers.*]

Already I am charged with treating this question, in the light of abstract ideas. I admit the charge, and would to heaven that this whole nation could now be brought to view it in the same calm, clear light. The failure so to view it is the one great national mistake. Our wise men and statesmen have insisted upon viewing the whole subject of the Negro upon what they are pleased to call practical and common sense principles, and behold the results of their so-called practical wisdom and common sense! Behold, how all to the mocker has gone.

Under this so-called practical wisdom and statesmanship, we have had sixty years of compromising servility on the part of the North to the slave power of the South. We have dishonored our manhood and lied in our throats to defend the monstrous abomination. Yet this greedy slave power, with every day of his shameless truckling on our part became more and more exacting, unreasonable, arrogant and domineering, until it has plunged the country into a war such as the world never saw before, and I hope never will see again.

Having now tried, with fearful results, the wisdom of reputed wise men, it is now quite time that the American people began to view this question in the light of other ideas than the cold and selfish ones which have hitherto enjoyed the reputation of being wise and practicable, but which are now proved to be entirely and absolutely impracticable.

The progress of the nation downward has been rapid as all steps downward are apt to be.

First. We found the Golden Rule impracticable.

Second. We found the Declaration of Independence very broadly impracticable.

Third. We found the Constitution of the United States, requiring that the majority shall rule, is impracticable.

Fourth. We found that the union was impracticable. The golden rule did not hold the slave tight enough. The Constitution did not hold the slave tight enough. The Declaration of Independence did not hold the slave at all, and the union was a loose affair and altogether impracticable. Even the Democratic Party bowed and squatted lower than all other parties, became at last weak and impracticable, and the slaveholders broke it up as they would an abolition meeting. [*Cheers.*] Nevertheless: I am aware that there are such things as practicable and impracticable, and I will not ignore the objections, which may be raised against the policy which I would have the nation adopt and carry out toward my enslaved and oppressed fellow countrymen.

There are at least four answers, other than mine, floating about in the public mind, to the question what shall be done with the Negro.

First. It is said that the white race can, if they will, reduce the whole colored population to slavery, and at once make all the laws and institutions of the country harmonize with that state of facts and thus abolish at a blow, all distinctions and antagonisms. But this mode of settling the question, simple as it is, would not work well. It would create a class of tyrants in whose presence no man's liberty, not even the white man's liberty would be safe. The slaveholder would then be the only really free man of the country—all the rest would be either slaves, or be poor white trash, to be kept from between the wind and our slaveholding nobility. The non-slaveholder would be the patrol, the miserable watchdog of the slave plantation.[52]

Second. The next and best defined solution of our difficulties about the Negro is colonization, which proposes to send the Negro back to Africa where his ancestors came from. This is a singularly pleasing dream. But as was found in the case of sending missionaries to the moon, it was much easier to show that they might be useful there, than to show how they could be got there. It would take a larger sum of money than we shall have to spare at the close of this war, to send five millions of American-born people, five thousand miles across the sea.

It may be safely affirmed that we shall hardly be in a condition at the close of this war to afford the money for such costly transportation [*cheers*], even if we could consent to the folly of sending away the only efficient producers in the largest half of the American union.

Third. It may be said as another mode of escaping the claims of absolute justice, [that] white people may emancipate the slaves in form yet retain them as slaves in fact just as General Banks is now said to be doing in Louisiana,[53] or then may free them from individual

---

52 The *Eagle* summarized the point of this paragraph as follows: "By this course an aristocracy would be founded, which would be intimately more dangerous to the liberties of the white man than ever the Negro was troublesome."

53 In January 1863, Union General Nathaniel P. Banks issued General Order No. 12, which created a system of sharecropping in Louisiana. The order stated that "all the conditions of continuous and faithful service" would be "enforced on the part

masters, only to make them slaves to the community. They can make of them a degraded caste. But this would be about the worst thing that could be done. It would make pestilence and pauperism, ignorance and crime, a part of American institutions. It would be dooming the colored race to a condition indescribably wretched and the dreadful contagion of their vices and crimes would fly like cholera and small pox through all classes. Woe, woe! to this land, when it strips five millions of its people of all motives for cultivating an upright character. Such would be the effect of abolishing slavery, without conferring equal rights. It would be to lacerate and depress the spirit of the Negro, and make him a scourge and a curse to the country. Do anything else with us, but plunge us not into this hopeless pit.

Fourth. The white people of the country may trump up some cause of war against the colored people, and wage that terrible war of races which some men even now venture to predict, if not to desire, and exterminate the black race entirely. They would spare neither age nor sex. *Even here in Brooklyn colored men have been hunted from their honest labor for no other cause than the color of their skin.*[54]

---

of the Negroes by the officers of the Government." Abolitionists sharply criticized Banks's action. See Philip S. Foner, ed., *The Life and Writings of Frederick Douglass*, Vol. 3 (New York: International Publishers, 1952), 442.

54 Douglass was almost certainly referring to the Tobacco Factory Riot of August 1862. According to the *New York Times*, a mob of over four hundred Irishmen attacked twenty black workers—mostly women and children—at a factory on

But is there not some chosen curse, some secret thunder in the stores of heaven red with uncommon wrath to blast the men who harbor this bloody solution? The very thought is more worthy of demons than of men. Such a war would indeed remove the colored race from the country—but it would also remove justice, innocence and humanity from the country. It would fill the land with violence and crime, and make the very name of America a stench in the nostrils of mankind. It would give you hell for a country and fiends for your countrymen. [*Cheers.*]

Now, I hold that there is but one way of wisely disposing of the colored race, and that is to do them right and justice. It is not only to break the chains of their bondage and accord to them personal liberty, but it is to admit them to the full and complete enjoyment of civil and political equality.

The mere abolition of slavery is not the end of the law for the black man, or for the white man. To emancipate the bondman from the laws that make him a chattel, and yet subject him to laws and deprivations which will inevitably break down his spirit, destroy his patriotism and convert him into a social pest, will be little gain to him and less gain to the country. One of the most plausible arguments ever made for slavery, is that

---

Sedgwick Street in Cobble Hill. Brooklyn's police force quickly stopped the assault, while the *Eagle* found the mob's actions "disgraceful." See the *New York Times* (August 5, 1862) and the *Eagle* (August 5, 1862).

which assumes that those who argue for the freedom of the Negro, do not themselves propose to treat him as an equal fellow citizen. The true course is to look this matter squarely in the face and determine to grant the entire claims of justice and liberty keeping back no part of the price.

But the question comes not only from those who hate the colored race, but from some who are distinguished for their philanthropy: can this thing be done? Can the white and colored people of America ever be blended into a common nationality under a system of equal laws? Mark, I state the question broadly and fairly. It respects civil and political equality, in its fullest and best sense: can such equality ever be practically enjoyed?

The question is not can there be social equality? That does not exist anywhere—there have been arguments to show that no one man should own more property than another. But no satisfactory conclusion has been reached. So there are those who talk about social equality, but nothing better on that subject than "*pursuit,*" the right of pursuit has been attained.

The question is not whether the colored man is mentally equal to his white brother, for in this respect there is no equality among white men themselves.

The question is not whether colored men will be likely to reach the presidential chair. I have no trouble here: for a man may live quite a tolerable life without ever breathing the air of Washington.

But the question is: Can the white and colored people of this country be blended into a common nationality, and enjoy together, in the same country, under the same flag, the inestimable blessings of life, liberty and the pursuit of happiness, as neighborly citizens of a common country?

I answer most unhesitatingly, I believe they can. In saying this I am not blind to the past. I know it well. As a people we have moved about among you like dwarfs among giants—too small to be seen. We were morally, politically and socially dead. To the eye of doubt and selfishness we were far beyond the resurrection trump. All the more because I know the past. All the more, because I know the terrible experience of the slave, and the depressing power of oppression, do I believe in the possibility of a better future for the colored people of America.

Let me give a few of the reasons for the hope that is within me.

The first is, despite all theories and all disparagements, the Negro is a man. By every fact, by every argument, by every rule of measurement, mental, moral or spiritual, by everything in the heavens above and in the earth beneath which vindicates the humanity of any class of beings, the Negro's humanity is equally vindicated. The lines which separate him from the brute creation are as broad, distinct and palpable, as those which define and establish the very best specimens of the Indo-Caucasian race. I will not stop here to prove the manhood of the Negro. His virtues and his vices, his courage and his cowardice, his beauties and his deformities, his wisdom and his folly, everything connected with him, attests his manhood.

If the Negro were a horse or an ox, the question as to whether he can become a party to the American government, and member of the nation, could never have been raised. The very questions raised against him confirm the truth of what they are raised to disprove. We have laws forbidding the Negro to learn to read, others forbidding his owning a dog, others punishing him for using firearms, and our Congress came near passing a law that a Negro should in no case be superior to a white man, thus admitting the very possibility of what they were attempting to deny.

The foundation of all governments and all codes of laws is in the fact that man is a rational creature, and is capable of guiding his conduct by ideas of right and wrong, of good and evil, by hope of reward and fear of punishment. Can any man doubt that the Negro answers this description? Do not all the laws ever passed concerning him imply that he is just such a creature? I defy the most malignant accuser to prove that there is a more law-abiding people anywhere than are the colored people. I claim for the colored man that he possesses all the natural conditions and attributes essential to the character of a good citizen. He can understand the requirements of the law and the reason of the law. He can obey the law, and with his arm and life defend and execute the law. The preservation of society, the protection of persons and property, are the simple and primary objects for which governments are instituted among men.

There certainly is nothing in the ends sought, nor in the character of the means by which they are to be attained, which necessarily excludes colored men. I see no reason why we may not, in time, co-operate with our white fellow-countrymen in all the labors and duties of upholding a common government, and sharing with them in all the advantages and glory of a common nationality.

That the interests of all the people would be promoted by the full participation of colored men in the affairs of government seems very plain to me. The American government rests for support, more than any other government in the world, upon the loyalty and patriotism of all its people. The friendship and affection of her black sons and daughters, as they increase in virtue and knowledge, will be an element of strength to the republic too obvious to be neglected and repelled. I predict, therefore, that under an enlightened public sentiment, the American people will cultivate the friendship, increase the usefulness and otherwise advance the interests of the colored race. They will be as eager to extend the rights and dignity of citizenship as they have hitherto been eager to deny those rights.

But a word as to objections. The Constitution is interposed. It always is.

Let me tell you something. Do you know that you have been deceived and cheated? You have been told that this government was intended from the beginning for white men, and for white men exclusively; that the men who formed the Union and framed the Constitution designed the permanent exclusion of the colored people from the benefits of those institutions. Davis, Taney and Yancey, traitors at the south, have propagated this statement, while their Copperhead echoes at the north have repeated the same.[55] There never was a bolder or more wicked perversion of the truth of history. So far from this purpose was the mind and heart of your fathers, that they desired and expected the abolition of slavery. They framed the Constitution plainly with a view to the speedy downfall of slavery. They carefully excluded from the Constitution any and every word which could lead to the belief that they meant it for persons of only one complexion.

The Constitution, in its language and in its spirit, welcomes the black man to all the rights which it was intended to guarantee to any class of the American people. Its preamble tells us for whom and for what it was made. But I am told that the ruling class in America

---

55 Jefferson Davis, Roger B. Taney, and William Yancey. Taney was the Supreme Court judge who wrote the *Dred Scott* decision (1857). Yancey was a leading secessionist who during the war served as Davis's emissary to England and France.

being white, it is impossible for men of color ever to become a part of the "body politic." With some men this seems a final statement, a final argument, which it is utterly impossible to answer. It conveys the idea that the body politic is a rather fastidious body, from which everything offensive is necessarily excluded. I, myself, once had some high notions about this body politic and its high requirements, and of the kind of men fit to enter it and share its privileges. But a day's experience at the polls convinced me that the "body politic" is not more immaculate than many other bodies. That in fact it is a very mixed affair.

I saw ignorance enter, unable to read the vote it cast. I saw the convicted swindler enter and deposit his vote. I saw the gambler, the horse jockey, the pugilist, the miserable drunkard just lifted from the gutter, covered with filth, enter and deposit his vote. I saw Pat, fresh from the Emerald Isle, requiring two sober men to keep him on his legs, enter and deposit his vote for the Democratic candidate amid the loud hurrahs of his fellow citizens. The sight of these things went far to moderate my ideas about the exalted character of what is called the body politic, and convinced me that it could not suffer in its composition even should it admit a few sober, industrious and intelligent colored voters. It is a fact, moreover, that colored men did at the beginning of our national history, form a part of the body politic, not only in what are now the free states, but also in the slave states. Mr.

William Goodell, to whom the cause of liberty in America is as much indebted as to any other one American citizen, has demonstrated that colored men formerly voted in eleven out of the thirteen original states.[56]

The war upon the colored voters, and the war upon the Union, originated with the same parties, at the same time, and for the same guilty purpose of rendering slavery perpetual, universal and all controlling in the affairs of the nation. Let this object be defeated and abandoned, let the country be brought back to the benign objects set forth in the preamble of the Constitution, and the colored man will easily find his way into the body politic, and be welcome in the jury box as well as at the ballot box. I know that prejudice largely prevails, and will prevail to some extent long after slavery shall be abolished in this country, but the power of prejudice will be broken when slavery is once abolished. There is not a black law on the statute book of a single free state that has not been placed there in deference to slavery existing in the slave states.

But it is said that the Negro belongs to an inferior race. Inferior race! This is the apology, the philosophical and ethnological apology for all the hell-black crimes ever committed by the white race against the blacks and the warrant for the repetition of those crimes through

---

56 William Goodell, a leading white abolitionist editor, was a founder of the Liberty Party in 1840 and ran as its candidate for president in 1852. Free blacks could vote in all of the thirteen original states except Georgia and South Carolina.

all times. Inferior race! It is an old argument. All nations have been compelled to meet it in some form or other since mankind have been divided into strong and weak, oppressors and oppressed. Whenever and wherever men have been oppressed and enslaved, their oppressors and enslavers have in every instance found a warrant for such oppression and enslavement in the alleged character of their victims. The very vices and crimes which slavery generates are usually charged as the peculiar characteristic of the race enslaved. When the Normans conquered the Saxons, the Saxons were a coarse, unrefined, inferior race. When the United States wants to possess herself of Mexican territory, the Mexicans are an inferior race. When Russia wants a share of the Ottoman Empire, the Turks are an inferior race, the sick man of Europe. So, too, when England wishes to impose some new burden on Ireland, or excuse herself for refusing to remove some old one, the Irish are denounced as an inferior race. But this is a monstrous argument.

Now, suppose it were true that the Negro is inferior instead of being an apology for oppression and proscription, it is an appeal to all that is noble and magnanimous in the human soul against both. When used in the service of oppression, it is as if one should say, "That man is weak; I am strong, therefore I will knock him down, and as far as I can I will keep him down. Yonder is an ignorant man. I am instructed, therefore I will do what I can to prevent his being instructed and to withhold from him the means of education. There is another who is low in his associations, rude in his manners, coarse and brutal in his appetites, therefore I will see to it that his degradation shall be permanent, and that society shall hold out to him no motives or incitements to a more elevated character." I will not stop here to denounce this monstrous excuse for oppression. That men can resort to it shows that when the human mind is once completely under the dominion of pride and selfishness, the reasoning faculties are inverted if not subverted.

I should like to know what constitutes inferiority and the standard of superiority. Must a man be as wise as Socrates, as learned as Humboldt, as profound as Bacon, or as eloquent as Charles Sumner,[57] before he can be reckoned among superior men? Alas! if this were so, few even of the most cultivated of the white race could stand the test. Webster was white and had a large head, but all white men have not large heads. The Negro is black and has a small head, but all Negroes have not small heads. What rule shall we apply to all these heads? Why this: Give all an equal chance to grow.

But I am told that the Irish element in this country is exceedingly strong, and that that element will never allow colored men to stand upon an equal political foot-

---

57 Sumner, a senator from Massachusetts, was a leading member of the abolitionist Radical Republicans.

ing with white men. I am pointed to the terrible out-
rages committed from time to time by Irishmen upon
Negroes. The mobs at Detroit, Chicago, Cincinnati, and
New York, are cited as proving the unconquerable aver-
sion of the Irish towards the colored race.

Well, my friends, I admit that the Irish people
are among our bitterest persecutors. In one sense it is
strange, passing strange, that they should be such, but
in another sense it is quite easily accounted for. It is said
that a Negro always makes the most cruel Negro driver,
a Northern slaveholder the most rigorous master, and
the poor man suddenly made rich becomes the most
haughty insufferable of all purse-proud fools. Daniel
O'Connell[58] once said that the history of Ireland might
be traced like a wounded man through a crowd—by the
blood. The Irishman has been persecuted for his religion
about as rigorously as the black man has been for his
color. The Irishman has outlived his persecution, and I
believe that the Negro will survive his.

But there is something quite revolting in the idea of a
people lately oppressed suddenly becoming oppressors,
that the persecuted can so suddenly become the persecutors. Let us see a small sample of the laws by which
our Celtic brothers have in other days been oppressed.
Religion, not color, was the apology for this oppression,

---

58 Leading nineteenth-century figure in the Irish independence movement.
During his travels in Ireland in 1845, Douglass became friends with O'Connell.

and the one apology is about as good as the other . . .[59]

Slavery has overleapt itself—having taken the sword it is destined to perish by the sword, and the long despised Negro is to bear an honorable part in the salvation of himself and the country by the same blow. It has taken two years to convince the Washington government of the wisdom of calling the black man to participate in the gigantic effort now making to save the country. Even now they have not fully learned it—but learn it they will, and learn it they must before this tremendous war shall be ended. Massachusetts, glorious old Massachusetts, has called the black man to the honor of bearing arms, and a thousand are already enrolled.

Now what will be the effect? Suppose colored men are allowed to fight the battles of the Republic. Suppose they do fight and win victories as I am sure they will, what will be the effect upon themselves? Will not the country rejoice in such victories? And will it not extend to the colored man the praise due to his bravery? Will not the colored man himself soon begin to take a more hopeful view of his own destiny?[60]

All the oppression and prejudice against the Negro

---

59 Douglass then provided a lengthy rundown of England's legal oppression of Catholics in Ireland.

60 The version of the speech printed in *Frederick Douglass' Monthly* next offered up a boilerplate conclusion: "Tonight we stand at the portals of a new world, a new life and a new destiny. We have passed through the furnace and have not been consumed. We have illustrated the fact that the two most opposite races of men known to ethnological science can . . . enjoy liberty, equality and fraternity in a common country." The *Eagle's* account recorded a more passionate finale.

*at the North arises simply from the fact that you op-
press us; do us justice, and when you begin to do this,
you will begin to like us. There is not much prejudice
against color now, because in coming down Broadway
the other day I saw a white lady riding by the side of a
colored man—it was true the colored man had a bit of
tinsel around his hat, but nobody seemed to notice it
and the lady did not show any signs of disgust. A few
days since a white lady asked me to walk down Broadway with her, and insisted on taking my arm, [and] as
we went along everyone we met stared at us as if we
were some curious animals.[61] What was the reason the
people did not stare at the coachman in the same manner? Simply because he was a servant and I was walking in the capacity of a friend. By and by you will get
over all this nonsense. [Cheers.] You ought to see me in
London walking down Broadway with a white lady on
each arm, and no person stared at us as if they thought
it strange. It will soon be so here, and we will then be all
the nobler and better. [Cheers.]*

*The friends of the Negro have heretofore done him
injustice in giving him too much credit for the possession of lamb-like qualities but I think we are on the way
to reverse the judgment of Mrs. Harriet Beecher Stowe,
and show that the Negroes are not all Uncle Toms. The*

---

61 Douglass is echoing an earlier incident in June 1850, when he was walking
down Broadway arm in arm with two white women, setting off what he at the time
described as a "brutal assault" from an angry mob. See the *North Star,* June 13, 1850.

prejudice against color will melt away when we see the gallant 54th Regiment of Massachusetts, well officered and drilled, marching down Broadway timing their footsteps to the music of "John Brown Hymn."[62] *When we hurl our black brigade at the throat of this rebellion, then and not till then will we see it put down, because they will make haste to surrender in order that they may be exchanged as prisoners of war.*

[End of speech.]

After thanking the audience for their attention the speaker retired. The Hutchinson family again sang some of their charming songs, and a gentleman in the audience stated that the colored child christened last week in Plymouth Church was in the audience, and as the audience would no doubt like to see it, he suggested that it should be placed upon the platform. The child, a bright intelligent-looking girl with auburn hair and as fair a complexion as any of the audience, was then placed on the stage and excited a good deal of admiration. Loud calls were made for Senator Pomeroy, but he declined to speak, and the audience dispersed after singing, with the Hutchinson family,

"John Brown's body lies moldering in the dust,
But his soul is marching on."

---

62 According to the *Brooklyn Daily Times* (May 16, 1863), Douglass also mentioned that his two sons, Lewis and Charles, were serving in the 54th Regiment.

❄

THE BROOKLYN DAILY EAGLE

MAY 16, 1863

THE AMALGAMATIONISTS SHOWING THEIR HAND.

Though we have no sympathy with the doctrines of the Abolition party, we are not without a great deal of respect for their perseverance and courage. They cannot be otherwise than sincere. In the face of a nation deluged with blood, in consequence of their agitation, they are exultant and joyous. Though in a minority today, they are so bold and so defiant that the majority cower before a faction so zealous and so resolute. Their success has been commensurate with their zeal, and they are no longer under the necessity of disguising their filthy purpose. They can stand before intelligent and cultivated women and advocate an amalgamation of the black and white races, though every instinct of their hearers recoil from it, and nature herself forbids the banns.[63]

By rapid degrees the control of the Republican Party is passing from the hands of the abolitionists into that of the amalgamationists. Or rather the abolitionists who have for some time controlled it have cast the disguise they assumed in deference to public sentiment and to public decency, and now appear in their true character.

---

63 Archaic term referring to "bonds" of marriage.

The first Republican club organized in this city claims as its founder Theodore Tilton, a protege of Rev. Mr. Beecher, and to him is fairly due the additional distinction of being one of the first American white men who would degrade his race by commingling its blood with that of the Negro, and leaving it to nature to impose the punishment the union merits in degradation, sterility and decay.

[The leading abolitionist] Mr. Wendell Phillips draws the outline of a picture, which it will not be his fault if we cannot contemplate without the trouble of going to Paris. "French civilization (we quote from Mr. Phillips)," rises above race. "At 5 o'clock, on the Boulevards, he had seen couples, black and white, promenading, and he himself was the only man uncivil enough to stare at them." And this is the future which our Beechers and Tiltons are laboring to work out for the sisters and daughters of American white men!

A meeting was held at the Academy of Music in this city last evening, presided over by the chief federal office holder in this city, at which a Negro advocated for his race the same privilege, and who threatened us with perpetual war unless we admit the Negro "to the most perfect political and social equality." When sentiments like these secure applause in Brooklyn from an audience made up of white men and women, we see no reason why the amalgamationists should despair of being able to reproduce here the mongrel breed who inhabit Central America, and who are only more despicable than the Negro, because even the Negro suffers from the unnatural amalgamation.

Mr. Frederick Douglass was the spokesman at the Academy last evening. He, like Mr. Tilton, thinks that because other nations were oppressed and enslaved, and won their way to social equality, that the darkey may do likewise. He instances the case of the Irish race, who were held to be the natural bondsmen of the English. The difference between the two cases is the difference between truth and falsehood. Individuals of the Irish race shone out as the starlight in the night time of her desolation, the peers in eloquence and in song, in arms and in arts—of the men of the race who claimed the right of oppressing them. Has the black race any such record to show? While in one case, eight hundred years of a history is a continued struggle for freedom; in the other the abject submission of a race who are content to be enslaved when there is an opportunity to be free, gives the best evidence that they are fulfilling the destiny which Providence marked out for them, when it stamped the marks of their inferiority on every joint from head to heel. For this filthy doctrine from Douglass, the colored man, there is some excuse: the white blood which flows in his veins has raised him above his races, but for the Tiltons who are anxious to degrade themselves we can find no extenuation.

The fanatical crusade which has in a few years

brought so many calamities upon a great country, appears now in all its naked deformity. By this false philanthropy the world knows what we have suffered. It is for the American people now to determine if the Tiltons, the Beechers and the Greeleys are to have the privilege of finishing their program. If we follow such leadership we are fit to be compared only to the quasi-apes their doctrine would develop.

Chapter 4

EMANCIPATION JUBILEE

Bedford-Stuyvesant

August 1865

In the first summer after the downfall of the Confederacy, African Americans across the land were more upbeat, and ready to celebrate. Yet in New York City, their prior efforts to do so had sparked controversy.

Just a few weeks after Robert E. Lee's surrender in April 1865, the New York Common Council had denied blacks the right to formally participate in Lincoln's funeral procession. At a Cooper Union event in early June, an indignant Douglass called the council's action "the most disgraceful and scandalous proceeding ever exhibited by people calling themselves civilized."[64]

But on Tuesday, August 1, Douglass and many members of Manhattan's African American population were in a far better mood as they traveled across the East River for an "Emancipation Jubilee" in Brooklyn.

---

64 See Theodore Hamm, "New York City's Juneteenth," *New York Daily News*, June 1, 2015.

And though he spoke only for a few minutes at the gathering, Douglass again memorably captured the spirit of the moment.

The jubilee was timed to coincide with West Indian Emancipation Day, which marked the end of slavery in the British Empire in 1834. Initially celebrated in abolitionist centers like Philadelphia, Boston, and Upstate New York, by the 1850s Emancipation Day events could be found across the frontier, from Indiana to California.

Douglass had regularly attended such events near his home in Rochester, but he hadn't yet journeyed down to Brooklyn for one of the local jubilees, which had been held regularly since the early 1850s. Everyone knew that the first one after the Civil War would be grand, though.

The August 1 festivities took place at two no-longer-extant places in what is currently Bedford-Stuyvesant—Adam Hanft's vast Myrtle Avenue Park (near Broadway)[65] and the smaller Lefferts Park (at Gates and Tompkins). At the time, the area was considered to be either part of the Eastern District (or greater Williamsburgh) or simply labeled East New York.

Despite their racist caricatures of "exultant darkies" or "dancing darkies," lengthy accounts in the Demo-

---

65 In his *Tribune* account Sydney Howard Gay noted, "This park is really a beautiful place. It comprises about twenty acres of lovely groves and five acres of lawn. Mosey banks everywhere invite you to recline upon the greensward and pillow your head upon them." All newspapers accounts about the jubilee cited in this chapter are dated August 2, 1865.

cratic *Eagle* and the Republican *New York Times* conveyed the mood of the attendees. "Twenty thousand men, women and children of sable hue yesterday mingled their joys and experiences in the suburban parks of the city of churches," said the *Times*. At stands outside Myrtle Avenue Park, the *Eagle* reported, "quaint-looking damsels in gorgeously striped dresses with brilliant turbans on their heads" dispensed peaches and pigs feet, with sides of corn, cabbage, apple dumplings, and chicken pot pie.

Writing in Horace Greeley's *New York Tribune*, editor Sydney Howard Gay maintained a more genteel tone. "Colored people" turned out in great numbers in their "Sunday best," Gay noted. He described a range of activities on display, including formal dancing in the Myrtle pavilion, as well as less highbrow amusements like a Jefferson Davis knockdown game, with three tosses costing a nickel.

In addition to live bands, carnival attractions, and sporting events (including a game played by the Weldenken Colored Baseball Club of Williamsburgh), there were also talks given by an array of distinguished African American speakers. At Myrtle, Professor William Howard Day (who had challenged segregation in Michigan in the late 1850s) explained the history of West Indian emancipation; while at Lefferts, Reverends James Pennington and James Gloucester urged receptive listeners to continue the fight for full equality.

When Douglass addressed the Myrtle gathering, the great orator was surprisingly brief. But what he said was also surprising, as illustrated by the divergent reports found in the various daily newspapers.

By all accounts, Douglass cheerfully told the enthusiastic crowd, "No man here wants to know whether liberty is a good thing or slavery a bad thing; we all know it already; we don't want any instruction." After all, he said, the main message of abolitionists had always been that "'every man is his own master; every man belongs to himself.'"

But what Douglass said next remains open to dispute. According to the *Times* (and the *Eagle*), he stated, "Every man has the right to do as he pleases, to come and go, to make love, get married, and do all sorts of things that are pleasant and profitable. [*Applause.*] We are here to enjoy ourselves—to sing, dance and make merry. I am not going to take up your time; go on; enjoy yourselves. [*Prolonged cheering.*]" The *Tribune* account by Douglass's friend Sydney Gay, however, says nothing about love or marriage, and skips right to "[W]e are here . . . to sing, dance and make merry."

Perhaps the most convincing reportage can be found in the *New York Herald*. James Gordon Bennett's paper—which had the largest circulation in the US—may have been a house organ of the War Democrats, who supported the Union yet opposed Lincoln, but during the Civil War, the paper bolstered its journalistic reputation by sending numerous correspondents into the field.

Near the end of its lengthy August 2, 1865, recap of the preceding day's jubilee events, the *Herald* presented Douglass's statements as follows:

> *The only thing abolitionists ever taught the American people was that every man is himself. That is all. Every man belongs to himself—can belong to nobody else. We are not here for in-struction. We are here to enjoy ourselves, to play ball, to dance, to make merry, to make love* [laughter and applause], *and to do everything that is pleasant. I am not going to take up your time. Go on, and enjoy yourselves.*

The moral instruction to "get married" is conspic-uously absent here. Yet of the various reports, the *Herald*'s is the one that most reads like an impromptu direct address. Such carefree comments by Douglass ultimate-ly seem most befitting an ecstatic daylong jubilee, one filled with joy in every sense of the word.

Beyond simply playful encouragement, Douglass in his brief remarks urged African Americans in Brooklyn and elsewhere to start envisioning their own future, and to fully enjoy their freedom. In the summer after the war, blacks everywhere could echo Douglass's insistence that, at last, "every man belongs to himself."

❋

THE BROOKLYN DAILY EAGLE

THURSDAY EVENING, 21 SEPTEMBER 1865

TRIUMPH OF JACKSON AND SPOONER

To the Editor of the Brooklyn Eagle:[66]

In looking over your issue of yesterday I noticed a report of cases tried at the City Court, in which an American citizen of African descent figured as a juryman—the first ever known in Brooklyn. We Brooklynites, ought certainly to feel proud that we were the first community to practically recognize the equality of the black man. No doubt a great many of the white trash will croak at such a thing, but, sir, the enlightened will rejoice that the Negro, who has cost the nation the lives of hundreds of thousands of white men and hundreds of millions of dollars to free him from bondage, can now take his place in the halls of justice as the peer of his white brother.

Now I, as a liberty-loving citizen, can see no living reason why we cannot fill our National and State offices with intelligent Negroes. By nominating a sound black ticket we could take the wind out of the sails of the white politicians who are endeavoring to foist into

---

66 As the *Eagle* reported on September 19, 1865, William Jackson was chosen as Brooklyn's first black juror by Jury Commissioner Alden Spooner, who was also a member of the Long Island Historical Society (now the Brooklyn Historical Society).

office such men as John Van Buren, Gen. Slocum, *et id genus omne* [and this sort of thing].[67]

By all means, Mr. Editor, get us up a colored ticket and while you are about it, why not place at the head of your paper the name of Frederick Douglass, black man, for the Presidency.

Yours, in a spirit of fraternity and equality,

"NIGER."

P.S.—Please hand down to immortality the names of the "Eleven," who had the sublime moral courage to act as fellow jurors with Jackson. *O tempora! O mores!*[68]

---

67 John Van Buren was the second son of President Martin Van Buren, and a prominent War Democrat in New York City; Henry W. Slocum, a Union general at Gettysburg, was a leading Brooklyn War Democrat.

68 Quote from Cicero meaning, *Oh the times! Oh the customs!*

CHAPTER 5

THE ASSASSINATION AND ITS LESSONS

Brooklyn Academy of Music
January 1866

D uring the summer and fall of 1865, Douglass urged his abolitionist and black audiences to continue the fight for equality—specifically by securing the right to vote for freedmen in the South. Full access to the ballot box, Douglass maintained, was even more important than land reform.[69]

At the same time, the biggest impediment to securing black equality was President Andrew Johnson, the Tennessee War Democrat who Lincoln had made part of his National Union Party ticket in the 1864 campaign. Despite his previous pledges as vice president to punish Confeder-

---

69 Unlike the Radical Republicans Thaddeus Stevens and Charles Sumner, Douglass did not call for a massive redistribution of land in the South (a plan better known as "Forty Acres and a Mule"). Instead, he insisted that political equality was a necessary first step in order to protect all gains for blacks. (He also viewed private property as sacrosanct.) After the end of Reconstruction in 1877, Douglass came to view his earlier position as incorrect, arguing that land reform would have secured economic independence for blacks. See Waldo E. Martin Jr., *The Mind of Frederick Douglass* (Charlotte: University of North Carolina Press, 1985), 68–72.

ate traitors, Johnson welcomed them back into the Union after Lincoln's death. And beginning in December of 1865, he sought to implement Presidential Reconstruction—without securing blacks' right to vote or ending the restrictive Black Codes passed by Southern states.

In response, historian Philip Foner observes, "During January and February, 1866, Douglass journeyed thousands of miles warning the people" regarding Johnson's policies. And, as Foner notes, the most notable stop on that tour was Brooklyn.[70]

Support for the War Democrats remained strong in the city[71]—and in both Brooklyn and New York City, many leading Republican opponents of the Confederates now rallied behind Johnson. That roster included Horace Greeley, the *New York Times,* and Henry Ward Beecher.

It was most likely Beecher's influence that sparked the controversy surrounding Douglass's speech at the Brooklyn Academy of Music in late January of 1866. Initially, BAM's directors denied Douglass's right to speak, on the utterly spurious grounds that the stage was not open to blacks, his May 1863 speech notwithstanding. As his steadfast friend and ally Theodore Tilton told

---

70 Foner, *Life and Writings,* Vol. 4, 18–19.

71 In the 1860 and 1864 elections, Lincoln lost in Brooklyn by wide margins. (The same was true in Manhattan, although Lincoln still carried New York State both times.) During the war, Brooklyn's mayor was Martin Kalbfleisch, a Bushwick chemical magnate and War Democrat. Elected to Congress in 1863, Kalbfleisch voted against the Thirteenth Amendment. Brooklyn had Republican mayors from 1864–1866, but Kalbfleisch's return to City Hall from 1867–1871 showed the enduring influence of the War Democrats.

the packed auditorium on January 29, a groundswell of support for Douglass had forced a full vote of the board, which came out 11–5 in the speaker's favor.

When he took the stage (before an almost entirely white audience), Douglass was in no mood to forgive the initial insult. But his speech that night was noteworthy for more than just his rhetorical assaults on BAM, Beecher, and Andrew Johnson. "The Assassination and Its Lessons" also demonstrated the full range of Douglass's dazzling oratorical abilities—as the speech was by turns caustic, illuminating, and poetic. Here is the *Eagle*'s account, followed by two contrasting responses.

❈

THE BROOKLYN DAILY EAGLE

JANUARY 30, 1886

A COLORED ORATOR AT THE ACADEMY.

MR. FRED. DOUGLASS ON THE "ASSAS-
SINATION AND ITS LESSONS."

Bitter Satire and Fierce Attack
on President Johnson.

WHAT THE NEGRO RACE THINK OF
"MOSES" AND THE PROMISED LAND.

SEVERE ON REV. MR. BEECHER.

Free Talk about the Reconstruction Question.

PRESIDENT JOHNSON HISSED.

Every seat in the Academy was filled, last evening to hear Mr. Frederick Douglass speak on "The Assassination and Its Lessons."

The audience numbered at least three thousand well-dressed people, about one half of whom were ladies. One or two colored men could be discovered in the body of the house and three sat on the stage, two of whom, Revs. [James Morris] Williams and [Joshua] Woodlin, are well-known and widely-esteemed Methodist Episcopal ministers of this city.

At 8 o'clock, Mr. Douglass, accompanied by Mr. Theodore Tilton, entered upon the stage. The moment the orator of the evening appeared, volley after volley of applause rolled through the building until the roof rang again with the echoes.

Mr. Tilton, advancing to the front of the stage, first gave notice of the Brooklyn Fraternity course of lectures—Feb. 6, Carl Schurz[72]; February 13, Wendell Phillips; February 20, Henry Ward Beecher; February 27, William Lloyd Garrison [*applause*]. I am glad, he continued, that you cheer the announcement, for I think that four such names make that problem which we used to hunt for when school boys—a four-leaved clover [*laughter*]. I am requested by Mr. Righter, chairman of the committee of this evening, in view of the various

---

72 German-born revolutionary who became a leading figure in the Republican Party. Although he was a decorated Union general and opponent of Johnson, Schurz was not a proponent of black equality.

statements made concerning the difficulties in procuring this house for Mr. Douglass tonight, to make a statement of the simple facts of the case.

Several weeks ago a number of gentlemen in this city who were desirous of giving Mr. Douglass a hearing before the people of Brooklyn applied to the directors of the Academy for the use of this platform tonight. After some delay, the answer which was reported was that the platform would be refused to him. In addition to that refusal, a director made another statement to the effect that no person of my friend's complexion would ever be allowed to speak in this house. [*Hisses.*] Well, of course the committee was not satisfied with that decision; the nobler-minded men among the directors were not satisfied with that decision. An appeal of the full case was made to the full board of directors. An animated debate was held. I am sorry to say that the result of that debate was not a unanimous vote, for that would have been just. Notwithstanding, the vote was in favor of allowing Mr. Douglass to speak, 11 to 5. [*Cheers.*] Yes, it is worthy of your applause. And yet the fact still stands that it is against the voted wish of one-third of the directors of this building that Mr. Douglass stands here tonight. Yet, although he has received from the directors of the Academy a divided welcome, you will present him with a united welcome. [*Applause.*] Sir [*turning to Mr. Douglass*], I know that that is the welcome you will receive; go and receive it.

The enthusiasm of the audience again burst out, even before the last sentence had been uttered. When silence was restored, a gentleman in the parquet stood up and said: What is the objection to his speaking?

Mr. Tilton: Because of his color, I suppose. Sir, I know not the reason. There are some things that ought not to be mentioned among you, as becometh the saints.[73] [*Loud laughter and applause.*]

Mr. Frederick Douglass then came forward and said:

I thank you very sincerely for this welcome, and all the more as I take it, or regard it, as a telling rebuke to the contemptible feeling which induced parties to object to my appearing here. The spirit that would drive me from this platform, if allowed, would drive me from the face of the earth; and if it had control in any other world than this, and it were possible for me to get into any other world than this, it would drive me thence. It's a mean spirit altogether, too mean for so large a city as is Brooklyn; and the day is coming when Brooklyn will be quite ashamed that any such objection could have been made, to a man's appearing before an audience in it for the purpose of vindicating the cause of justice, of humanity and of liberty. [*Applause.*]

How the World Progresses

I am to speak to you, this evening, on "The Assassina-

---

73 A swipe at Beecher.

tion and Its Lessons." I would disclaim, however, at the outset the office of teacher, implied in the title of my subject. The world has made some progress, is making progress, and will make more by and by, but it has been indebted for whatever progress it has made to two kinds of teachers: first great men; and, secondly, great events. Great men, by virtue of their endowments, are able often to determine future results, grand results from very occult beginnings, and inferences from principles. But the natural and most effective schoolmaster of nations is great events. They teach on a broad and a grand scale those lessons of justice, of liberty, and of national honor, without the observance of which no nation can be really prosperous or pre-eminently great. The masses of men being in the great struggle of life—for with the masses the whole struggle is to live—have little time or attention to give to theories of any sort, or help to distinguish between good and bad principles by their results. Few understand the rule and the reason for it. Many seem to require an illustration—palpable, visible, arising and often startling—before they can be instructed.

Long before our goodly land was torn and rent as it has been by the giant footsteps of civil war, when success was ours and the elements apparently tranquil, and no danger menaced the national safety at any point, a few men amongst us—good, true men—stood by the side of the degraded, of the outcast of society, the enslaved of our land. Looking up from that lowly position to the

source of eternal justice and goodness for life, they fore-
saw all the calamities which have since fallen upon our
land. They warned us, but we treated their warnings
as an idle tale. Thus hath it ever been! The tears of the
bondwoman standing on the auction block weeping for
her children sold and gone anointed the eyes of these
few, so that they saw clearly. But it was only the loud
thunders of Sumter and the social earthquakes which
have since followed that opened the dull eyes of the nation at large to the dangers arising out of the existence
of slavery—and to the dangers arising out of permitting
a privileged class in our midst.

The past year has been remarkable for two very instructive events. One of them brought to the national
heart unspeakable joy and gladness, for it was the sudden collapse, the downfall of a fierce, sanguinary and
formidable rebellion, undertaking to redress no wrongs.
It was an undertaking to assert no great human right,
as some rebellions have done, but solely to perpetuate
the ascendancy of a privileged class of men in one section of our country and to make perpetual the system
of slavery in that section. That was the object—and it
was thought, vainly hoped, and vehemently desired that
with the downfall of the rebellion these unspeakably
wicked objects would have been abandoned on the
part of the South and on the part of the North, and
that a privileged class would have been rendered impossible hereafter. Indeed, that all questions that have

disturbed us these thirty years past would have been settled, and settled so as to require no future settlement; settled in accordance with the genius of American institutions.

The other event to which I have referred, and which is to be the subject of this evening's discourse, filled the national heart with unspeakable anguish, bitterness and mortification. For it was the inauguration of a new crime in our land, a stranger to these latitudes, an alien to our institutions. Assassination of the nation's chief magistrate! We had heard of assassinations elsewhere, under other institutions. But we had not supposed that in the land where free institutions were established, where the right to vote and freedom of speech were general, that there could be anything amongst us to foment such a giant conspiracy as that disclosed by the assassination and the attempted wholesale assassinations at Washington.[74] We mourned and we are mourning his loss. We are now passing into another year, and it remains to be seen what this year may have in store for us. Many may feel hopeful and predict very favorable results from present indications, but from my standpoint, judging from the clouds that lower at this time on the political sky, I feel some fear, and have some apprehensions that this year may rival its predecessor by taking upon itself

---

74 John Wilkes Booth and his coconspirators initially planned to assassinate Lincoln, Andrew Johnson, and Secretary of State William Seward. Seward was wounded but not killed; the Johnson plan never came to fruition.

features even darker and more deplorable than either assassination or rebellion.

The crime of crimes which now threatens us is nothing less than the base and wanton betrayal by a triumphant nation of its only allies and friends, placing them back again into the hands of their common enemies. I say that this is what I apprehend and what the signs of the times, according to my outlook, threaten. But more of this by and by.

The American people ought to be instructed. They have suffered a great deal during this war. They have experienced many shakes, some of them heavy and terrible in the extreme, causing the very pillars of the state to tremble and the boldest hearts among us to quail in view of the possible future of the Republic. But the heaviest shock of all, the most instructive of all, was—

The Assassination of President Lincoln.
You all remember the effect produced by it. I cannot describe it; you cannot describe it; no man can describe the effect produced by that result. It was as if some grand convulsion in nature had occurred, as if the solid earth had opened, or the graves had burst beneath our feet. The consternation could not have been more profound. A hush fell upon the land—a solemn stillness, as if each man on it had heard a voice from heaven and paused to learn its meaning. The calamity was so sudden, so out of joint with the general sense of security. There unfolded

a transition so vast from one extreme of feeling to the other—from victory to the very dust and ashes of sorrow and mourning—that few among us could believe the dreadful news to be true.

As at no time before or during the war, the loyal people of the land were rejoicing in the great and decisive victories over the rebels. Richmond, so long besieged and so sternly and desperately defended, had fallen. Mobile and Wilmington were in our hands. South Carolina had received her proper chastisement at the hands of General Sherman. Everywhere we were victorious. The loyal armies were disbanded. Everywhere hopes of peace were indicated. Even General Lee, the patrician, with his so-called invincible army, made up of the elite of Virginia, had surrendered to General Grant, the plebian. [*Applause.*] Loyal black troops with iron arms and steel fingers were upholding our flag at Charleston and timing their footsteps to the tune of "Old John Brown." [*Applause.*]

At the same time the loyal people of the North were parting with their just indignation against the insolent rebels, and were beginning to speak of them no longer as deadly foes, but simply as our erring brothers. Southern generals were becoming decidedly popular all over the North. Lee was spoken of with as much respect as General Grant. But what did it avail? Whom did it appease? What Southern heart was softened? Was the Slave Power conciliated by it? I answer, no! It was not then, it is not now, and it never will be by such means. Nothing, nothing short of the iron hand of federal power will command respect. [*Applause.*] In the moment when the great North was laying aside its armor, sick of blood, weary of war; when the whole Northern sky was fringed with the golden hue of peace; when the whole North was meditating mercy towards the vanquished. In that moment, when nothing was to be gained by it, they gave us this indication of their deadly hate, manifesting this, their intense malignity, by striking their first blow at President Lincoln. They could not conquer, but they could [assassinate], thus showing the deadly spirit with which we have to contend.

Eulogy on the Late President.

From what I have now said you will readily perceive that I am not here for the purpose of treating you to a lecture on the life and character of our lamented president. That is already a well-trodden field. The pulpit, the platform, poetry and art in all their developments have been engaged since the hour of his death to illustrating the character of this good man, and in commending his virtues to the people. There is a charm, however, about the life of this man that will never lose its power over the American people—never! It will never grow old. A thousand years hence, when the solid marble that held his remains shall have crumbled; when hundreds of military heroes who have risen under his administration shall have been forgotten; when even the details of the late tremendous war shall have faded from the pages of history, and the war itself shall seem but as a speck up the long vista of ages, then Abraham Lincoln, like dear old John Brown, will find eloquent tongues to rehearse his history, and commend his philanthropy and virtues as a standard to the rulers of nations. Wherever freedom has an advocate, or humanity a friend, his name will be held as an auxiliary.

One thing about Abraham Lincoln will always make him dear to the struggles for fame. He was indebted to himself for himself—largely the architect of his own fortune. So far as man can be he was a self-made man. A worker, a toiler; the captain of a flat boat; a raftsman; a worker in wood, in iron, on the soil. A man who took life at the roughest, with brave hands grappled with it and conquered; a man who traveled far, but made the road on which he traveled; who ascended high, but built the ladder on which he climbed. Flung overboard as it were in the midnight storm and left without oars or life preservers, he swam in safety to shore, where other men would have despaired and gone down. [*Applause.*]

His life, however, requires a book rather than a lecture, and I don't intend to enter very fully upon it here. The position he occupied as the head of this government; the difficulties which beset him at the outset; the perils through which he passed; the singular purity of his life and the tragic manner of his death—all are matters upon which I might dwell to any length. But all men know Abraham Lincoln. No man was ever better known to the American people; they know him as they never knew any man before. They know of his good temper, which no insolence could disturb; they know of his numerous anecdotes; of his vigilance; of his remarkable trust in the people, walking among them without a guard when he was commander-in-chief of a million armed men. All know this, and more of him, more than I can say.

The Present Reconstruction System: A Warning.

The question arises: why take this man as the text of this occasion? I answer by underscoring the assassination of Abraham Lincoln, the manner of it and the causes leading to it. It is a warning that people have to care, lest in the Reconstruction which is now proposed with the South, we shall contract with coming generations for a repetition of this crime—and worse, the next crime would come to us legitimately, if we shall plant it as this was planted among us. I take this as the text from which to preach the lessons proper to this hour, given the dangers and doubts before us. We are indebted to our enemies, for while I have had boundless faith in the virtues of the North during the war, I have had more in the persistent villainy of the people of the South.

I will tell it how it is: history will write down the fact, discreditable to the present generation, that we have only taken stands towards public virtue when compelled to do so by some stupendous crime committed towards the North on the part of the South. It has been so for the last thirty years. The annexation of Texas; the passing of the Fugitive Slave Bill, intended to demoralize the people of the North, but producing a contrary effect; and the invasion of Kansas by border ruffians are instances in point. The hanging of John Brown called forth the indignation of the civilized world against slavery. Every step—every step—towards a right position has been necessary in consequence of some new outrage enacted by the Slave Power.

We are in the same scale tonight, and whether we come out of this contest with our hands clear, and these questions settled as they should be, depends still upon the behavior of the people of the South. Great and good as Abraham Lincoln was, had he died in a natural way we should have followed him to his grave—sadly to be sure but with little of that deep feeling manifested at his funeral. Dying as he did die, of course his very name became a text. Dying for good government as against anarchy; for loyalty as against reason; for liberty as against slavery—his death demands that every vestige of the cause that led to his assassination shall be utterly and forever blotted out. [*Applause.*] It asks that we not only shall lay the axe to the root of the tree, but that the whole tree, root and branch, shall be given to the flames. [*Applause.*] Not only that slavery shall be destroyed, but that liberty in its length and breadth shall be as supremely established as slavery before was dominant. [*Applause.*] The man who hereafter votes for a privileged class in any part of the country stamps upon the grave of Abraham Lincoln, insults his memory, and causes his wounds to bleed afresh.

Washington City Then and Now—A Contrast—
President Johnson Insults Loyal Black Soldiers.

It was my exceedingly great privilege to know Abraham Lincoln personally. I saw him often during the war and conversed with him freely on subjects connected with the suppression of the rebellion. I can say of him that I never met a man with whom I more readily felt myself at home. A true man. Never a man more solid, never a man more transparent. Some men have two sides, some more. Abraham Lincoln had but one side. Some men have a long side and a short side, an amiable side and a jolly side, but Abraham Lincoln was the same man from whichever side you viewed him. I have to say, that could he have lived to this hour, he would have stood today with the men who stand foremost—he would have gone today with the men who go foremost for the assertion of equal rights at the South as a condition of their representation in Congress.[75] [*Applause.*]

---

75 In response to Johnson's conciliatory Presidential Reconstruction, in early 1866 Radical Republicans, led by Senator Charles Sumner and Representative Thaddeus Stevens, initiated Congressional Reconstruction (also called Radical

Perhaps you would like to know how I came to visit Abraham Lincoln. I will tell you that, too. He invited me to the White House [*laughter and applause*]—and the fact that he could invite a black man to the White House is, itself, indicative of what would have been his course this day. Abraham Lincoln was a tall man. And the dawning of the truth touched his brow often a little earlier than it did the dwellers in the valley, than it did the diggers in the copper mines and other mines [*shouts of laughter and applause*]. He saw that this war was to inaugurate a new dispensation in these United States, and he saw it gratefully, joyfully. By inviting a Negro to visit him, Lincoln said, "I am president of all the people of the United States—not merely of white people, but of black people, and of all the people. And I regard the rights of all the people, and respect the feelings of all the people." It was a telling rebuke to popular prejudice that this man could invite the Negro not to the White House only, or to the soldiers' home, but to the table of the President of the United States [*applause*]—that Negro whom some of the directors of the Brooklyn Academy would have excluded from this building. [*Prolonged cheers and laughter.*]

I saw Mr. Lincoln, as I said, often. On one occasion, as I was visiting him—I tell this partly for my own benefit, partly for the benefit of the directors of this build-

---

Reconstruction). Black equality was central to this effort, as illustrated by the Civil Rights Bill of 1866 (which survived Johnson's veto) and the Fourteenth Amendment, passed in 1868.

ing just now spoken of [*laughter and applause*], and partly out of respect for the memory of our lamented president— Governor Buckingham[76] came and desired an interview with the president. "Tell the governor to wait," said the president. "I have my friend Douglass here, and I want to have a long talk with him." This was the first time, I think, when the president of the United States refused admission to the governor of a great state, while a Negro was with him, or when the governor of a little state on a similar occasion had to stand out in the cold. It was a telling rebuke to popular prejudice, and showed the moral courage of the man.

Many a man can march out on to the perilous edge of battle, but has not the moral courage to confront popular prejudice. Mr. Lincoln could do all this and do it in a manner that reflected credit upon himself, for he had this peculiarity, which was very peculiar at that time and is not altogether saved from singularity at the present moment. He could entertain and converse with a black man without once reminding him of the color of his complexion or any peculiarity whatever. On one occasion a well-known abolitionist of New York said to me, "Come, Douglass, let's walk down Broadway together. I'm never ashamed to walk with a Negro." It never occurred to him that I might be ashamed to walk with him. [*Roars of laughter.*]

---

76 Governor William A. Buckingham of Connecticut, a Republican and close Lincoln ally.

Washington has sadly deteriorated since Mr. Lincoln's death. Had he lived, loyal black troops would never have been insulted as they were a short time ago when they were told by Andrew Johnson to go anywhere, to do anything to prove that they are entitled to their freedom.[77] Is freedom, then, an experiment anywhere on this continent? To talk about freedom as an experiment! I had always thought that freedom was the normal condition of man and that slavery was an experiment. But Mr. Johnson, in addressing loyal black troops, tells them to go home and go to work, and prove that they are entitled to their freedom! I am quite willing to agree that all men should have work to do. Thackeray says that "all men are as lazy as they can afford to be"—and I suppose that in this respect the black man stands on a level with the rest of mankind. But let us have no invidious distinctions here. I hold that if to work is a virtue the black people of the South are the saints and their former masters are the sinners.

Mr. Johnson could have called that delegation [of former Confederates] from Georgia before him and said, "Why, gentlemen, complain of the Negro not working? I am aware that men are lazy, and all that; but you should remember that by striking at the life of this government you have lost your power to obtain a

---

77 In October 1865, President Johnson asked an assembly of black soldiers, "Will you give evidence to the world that you are capable and competent to govern yourselves? That is what you will have to do."

living by the work of other men. Instead of crying that 'the Negroes won't work; the Negroes won't work,' I advise you to pull off your jackets and go to work like honest men!" But as I said, he insulted the Negro. Insulted him, when it is remembered what the Negro has done in this war. Insulted these soldiers coming fresh from war, where they had slept on the cold ground in winter; where they had been storming forts; where they had been bearing all manner of hardships and dangers in the contest on behalf of the nation at large. Coming home, some of them were maimed, some of them mutilated; they were limping heroes from the battle, with banners torn and riven by the rifle shot of the enemy. Coming before the president for a "Well done good and faithful servant"—for a word of approval—instead they are told to go home and work to prove that they are entitled to freedom! Told this in a country where to be a man is to be entitled to "life, liberty and the pursuit of happiness!"

Negro Manhood.
These Negroes came into this contest on a higher plane of nobility than any other class that came into this war. I do not deny the magnanimity of your sons or your brothers. Not at all. There was never a white regiment that left my part of the country to enter into this contest that I did not follow with tearful eye. But I say that the Negro came into this contest on a higher plane than

any other class that entered into it. The Bible tells of the value of a man who will lay down his life for a friend, and that would be called true nobility. The Negro came into this contest not to lay down his life for his friends, but to lay down his life for those who had never been his friends. To lay down his life for a country that had rejected him, and that treated him as an alien. To lay down his life for a country that had scourged him as beyond the range of free institutions; for a country whose emblem or symbol excluded him from its outspread wings and refused to shelter him; for a country where his ancestry could be tracked by their blood droppings for 200 years. Yet, at the call of this country—when no honors were offered him; when the laws of war would not afford him any protection and he had less pay than other soldiers; when he fought in a halter—still he leaped to this contest and fought this battle to the last and fought it well. [*Applause.*]

Mr. Lincoln's Plan of Reconstruction.

I have said that Mr. Lincoln would have been in favor of the enfranchisement of the colored race. I tell you, he was a progressive man; he never took any step backwards. He did not begin by playing the role of Moses and end by playing that of Pharaoh; he began rather by playing Pharaoh and ending by that of Moses.[78] His

---

78 In October 1864, as military governor of Tennessee, Johnson had famously vowed, "I will indeed be your Moses, and lead you through the Red Sea of war and

last days were better than his first. He said to me that
he was in favor of the enfranchisement of two classes
of the Southern people. First, all those who had taken
any part in suppressing the rebellion; and secondly, all
those who could read and write.[79] He was in favor of the
enfranchisement of both these classes. It was like Mr.
Lincoln to feel his way thus. He was in favor of thus
extending the enfranchisement of the colored people of
the South. He told me so, over and over again. He had
learned statesmanship over the rail and the wedge. He
had learned to insert the thin edge of the wedge first. In
a letter to Gen. Wadsworth, he had said that in looking forward to Reconstruction he had two measures
in view: first, a universal amnesty to the people of the
South; second, universal suffrage to the blacks of the
South. These two propositions he looked forward to as
the main propositions which should enter into his plan
of Reconstruction, and I believe he would have carried
it out . . .[80]

---

bondage, to a fairer future of liberty and peace." By contrast, Lincoln had entered
the war as a mild opponent of slavery, yet increasingly became a strong one.

79 In his final speech (on April 11, 1865), Lincoln stated his belief that the right
to vote for freed blacks should be "conferred on the very intelligent, and on those
who serve[d] our cause as soldiers."

80 In a January 1864 letter to General James S. Wadsworth, an abolitionist
Republican from New York, Lincoln first stated, "I cannot see, if universal amnesty
is granted, how . . . I can avoid exacting in return universal suffrage, or, at least,
suffrage on the basis of intelligence and military service." That Lincoln was leaning
in the direction Douglass mentions was confirmed by his subsequent statement in
the letter that "the restoration of the Rebel States to the Union must rest upon the
principle of civil and political equality of both races."

General Banks has rather shrewdly said that republics have defective memories; someone else has said that republics are ungrateful. I fear both propositions may be proved by America just now. But why bring this subject up now when to forget or forgive is the popular cry, not only in Washington but also in Brooklyn? Christianity is a more liberal system of forgiveness, for if our brother trespasses seven times a day—even seventy times seven—we are to forgive him. Yes, but on one condition: that he repent. [*Laughter and applause.*] The Bible says, "If I regard iniquity in my heart, the Lord will not hear me." But it seems that we have a class of men among us who are disposed to forgive men whether they repent or not.

Sharp Attack on Mr. Beecher.
According to Mr. Johnson and Mr. Beecher, we are to forgive [the Confederates], and we are not to be impatient even if they don't repent right away. [*Laughter.*] I know a man who once preached "first pure, then peaceable," and I think when preaching this, he preached well. Now I find the same preacher preaching "first peaceable, then pure!" But I am not surprised at this because I once heard him say that if the question were submitted to him whether he would have slavery abolished immediately without the aid of the church, or wait 25 years and have it abolished by the church, he should be in favor of waiting. If he had been a slave, and I had

a decent sort of a slave whip in my hand and stood over him, I could have changed Mr. Beecher's opinion. [*Prolonged cheers and laughter*.] I think he would have been in favor of abolishing slavery whether the church were ready for it or not. [*Continued laughter*.]

We have learned a great deal by this war, but we have not learned quite enough. The nation must feel the sting of slavery a little deeper before it will be brought to do justice to the Negro. The plan now proposed at Washington for bringing back these states into the Union is, in my opinion, a most wanton and dishonorable abandonment of our allies, our only allies during this war. The Negro was our friend during the war—and such a friend. He was the only friend that the white soldier running away from Southern slave prisons desired to see. I wish that the American people could only be as true to freedom and to loyalty in this Reconstruction as the rebels proved themselves to be during all the war. Jefferson Davis was a great criminal—a cold-blooded traitor—a devouring wolf, but not a wolf in sheep's clothing, though he was found in other clothing.[81] Though a traitor, he was a constant traitor; though a felon, and awaiting a felon's punishment, he will never be punished.[82] There is

---

81 After Robert E. Lee's surrender in April 1865, Davis remained at large until his capture by Union soldiers at Irwinville, Georgia, one month later. Davis was wearing his wife's black shawl at the time he was nabbed, provoking endless ridicule in the Northern press.

82 Davis was not charged with treason. In 1867, a group of leading Northerners— including Cornelius Vanderbilt, Horace Greeley, and, most improbably, Gerrit

not persistent hatred of treason enough in this country to punish Jefferson Davis. The president persists in trying him by the only way in which he can be acquitted, and refuses to try him by any way in which he is likely to be punished. I wish I was as safe from railway accidents as Davis is from punishment. [*Laughter.*]

Davis was a constant traitor—true to his men. No man that ever fought under his piratical flag can say that he deserted his colors. True to the last, Davis stuck to the cause while there was anything left of it. But what shall be said of Mr. Johnson, the successor to Mr. Lincoln? What shall be said of him? Yes, what shall be said of Andrew Johnson? [*Hisses and cheers.*] Of the man who holds that treason is a crime and must be punished—that treason must be made odious by punishment? What shall be said of Andrew Johnson if instead of punishing traitors, he signalizes his administration by pardoning the guiltiest of traitors? What shall be said of him—who said to us that in the Reconstruction, which he proposed, traitors were to take back seats and loyal men front ones? What shall be said of him if in the Reconstruction, which he encourages, traitors and rebel generals are placed in the front seats and made provisional governors? One of these men said three days before he was appointed provisional gover-

Smith—helped post Davis's $100,000 bond, angering Radical Republican leaders. Some viewed Davis's legal limbo as providing the Confederates a rallying cry, but Smith believed that the responsibility for slavery ultimately lay in the North.

nor that no man at the South regretted the failure of the rebellion more than he. And yet such a man is called upon to shape the course of South Carolina.[83]

What shall be said of the man who said that he would be the Moses of the black race? What shall be said of him if he comes out in his inaugural address and says that in his opinion the Negroes will sooner receive their rights from their former masters than from Northern men, from loyal men? [*Cries of "Never" and "Shame."*] What shall be said of him if he intends to exalt our enemies and depress our friends—our only friends? A man who wants to enfranchise our enemies and disfranchise our friends? What shall be said of him if instead of accepting the opportunity of settling the Negro question forever, he hands it down to coming generations, to foster future rebellions and breed other assassinations? What shall be said of him if he does such wicked things—and thus dishonors the government and invites the contempt, scorn, and derision of an onlooking world?

The remainder of the orator's discourse expressed strong disappointment at broken promises—when suffrage was to follow the sword, and the ballot the bayonet, but had not . . . The speaker knew that the president had some sort of theological defense for

---

83 Although he was a Unionist prior to the rebellion, Benjamin Franklin Perry of South Carolina had become a staunch Confederate during the war. Johnson appointed him as provisional governor in June 1865.

his actions—"Once in grace, always in grace" meant "Once in the Union, always in the Union." He said that Johnson is trying to be metaphysical, theological, and everything else. [Laughter.]

The president says that the Confederate states were never out of the Union! Well, I don't know that I am able to answer him on this point, but one thing I know—that if these states were not out of the Union, the Union for four years was out of them. [*Renewed laughter.*] . . . We know that the Southern planter, with 10,000 acres of land over which he reigns like a monarch, cares nothing for the enfranchisement of the blacks. But if the Negro does not obtain equal rights, the community is going to be agitated, for while there is any injustice left, the black man will not keep silent.

[Mr. Douglass] would carry away from the meeting a very grateful feeling towards the citizens of Brooklyn for their kindness in coming to hear what he had to say that evening, and for the admirable rebuke which that large and intelligent audience was to miserable prejudice which would have excluded him from that hall.

Mr. Douglass spoke extempore, and occupied two hours and a quarter in the delivery of his address. Loud cries of "Tilton" and "speech" arising from the audience, that gentleman made a brief address, proposing in one glass of water the health of, first, Frederick Douglass, for his kindness in addressing them; second, of the eleven directors who permitted him to speak in that house; and third, of the "absent friends," the five directors who had lost the greatest treat of the season in not being present to hear all the audience has heard. He followed with some remarks on the same theme as the speaker who had just sat down.

A cry was raised in the audience of "three cheers for President Johnson." An attempt was made to give them but proved a total failure. A storm of hisses instantly arose, which were drowned in the storm of cheers that arose when someone called from the stage—"Three cheers for equal rights." The audience then quietly dispersed.

✸

The week after the BAM speech in 1866, Douglass traveled to Washington, DC, where he and other black leaders met with President Johnson. During the February 7 summit Johnson pompously reiterated his Moses claim, but then belittled the importance of black voting rights. He stated, "Suppose, by some magic touch, you could say to every [black man in the South], 'You shall vote tomorrow'—how much would that ameliorate their condition at this time?" When the president later proposed that blacks eager to change their conditions should emigrate to the North, Douglass reminded him that slave masters were again "making the laws, and we cannot get away from the plantation." In closing, Douglass made a strong case for full voting rights.[84]

The transcript of the meeting made it seem as though Douglass was forceful but not disrespectful in his direct conversation with Johnson. However, the *New York Times* took umbrage with Douglass's comments—and connected them back to his hostile comments toward the president at BAM. One day after the summit, the *Times* issued the following editorial, which is notable for its condescension towards Douglass as well as its hearty embrace of "Moses."

✳

The New-York Times.

FEBRUARY 8, 1866

THE PRESIDENT AND THE RIGHTS OF THE FREEDMEN.

The reported conversation with the president with a number of Negro gentlemen, which is given in another column, does not present anything which throws new light upon the executive policy. Mr. Frederick Douglass naturally entertains an exalted view of the past services and the future destinies of his race. He holds, indeed, as we gather from a recent speech which he delivered in Brooklyn, that but for the colored troops the issue of

---

84 For a transcript, see Foner, *Life and Writings*, Vol. 4, 182–191.

the late war would have been the triumph of the rebel cause. No one will think of blaming the representative man of the colored race for cherishing this view of the indispensable service rendered by the Negro troops in the great war. Although the majority of our loyal citizens may believe that the authority of the government might have been asserted by the stout arms and brave hearts of the race whose forefathers established a republican government on this continent, Mr. Frederick Douglass, it must be admitted, has found enough to justify whatever he may choose to arrogate for his kindred in the declarations of a variety of journals owned and controlled by people of a different complexion from himself. One of these journals, which is understood to have a great influence in religious circles, declares that, "except for the two hundred thousand muskets which the Negro added to the army of the Union, the Federal Congress might not have been able to sit today." And it adds: "Shall the Republic be ungrateful to *its preservers?*"[85]

The spokesman of the freed Negroes who reads such extravagant eulogy as this cannot well be blamed if he not only accepts the proffered homage on behalf of his race, but even goes the length of treating with ill-conceived contempt the labors, the endurance, and even the courage of such armies as won the grand *decisive* battle of Gettysburg, before a single Negro soldier

---

85 Italics in *New York Times* editorial. It's likely that the statement came from Tilton's *Independent*.

was seen east of the Alleghenies. That battle was the turning point of the war. The blow then struck Lee never recovered from. Such is the irreversible judgment of military men both North and South. And it is disputed now only by those (outside of the Negro communion) who are determined that the war between the North and the South shall be perpetual, and who are using, to that end, the poor deluded race that has just escaped from bondage.

For both the Negro and his selfish patrons, the president has words of warning and counsel which ought to be heeded. With nothing but kindness in his heart for the emancipated race—and promising to fulfill his pledge to be their "Moses"—the president tells them how vain and delusive, and how terribly perilous must be any attempt to secure their immediate enfranchisement against the universal opinion of those who must continue to be their employers. He shows that even in the District of Columbia the proposition to confer on them an unqualified suffrage right, awakens against them the sentiment of the entire white population. He points to the certainty of the same hostility to universal suffrage in the states where the black race is most numerous; and he warns them of the danger of the antagonisms that must follow any legislation which should array the one race against the other where slavery has long existed.

It is not at all to be expected that such judicious and

fatherly advice would be accepted in good spirit by a class who not only hold themselves to be the saviors of the nation, but who find a powerful faction both in and out of Congress clamorously asserting these preposterous claims on their behalf. Mr. Frederick Douglass would be more humble and unobtrusive than any apostle of his people that has yet appeared on the public stage, if he failed to profit by all that is conceded by the amalgamationists on behalf of the bravery and preeminent patriotism of his kindred. And he would have far less astuteness than usually belongs to his class if he did not use every confession which throws discredit on the loyal endurance of the white race, as so much leverage for his especial cause. We should hardly doubt, at the same time, that he must feel a fair share of contempt for such of the patrons of the Negro race as affect to sneer at their own kindred while magnifying its glory. And if he defiantly tells the president that he "appeals from him to the people," the Negro leader finds an exemplar in the revolutionists in Congress who threaten the executive with impeachment unless he bends before their decrees.

No one within the whole boundary of this republic has the welfare of the emancipated class at the South more thoroughly at heart than President Johnson. No one has worked with more sedulous care during those months of restored peace, to see that those whom the fortunes of war, and the constitutional enactments of the federal and state legislatures has freed from slavery, should be protected in the possession of the immunities thus acquired. Every step in the progress of Reconstruction was guarded by conditions which had their origin essentially in the determination to make freedom universal and impartial. [There is] nothing that could possibly bear upon the protection of the freedmen from injustice at the hands of their former masters . . . His course has not only been clearly marked out from the hour when he succeeded to the presidency, but it has been followed with steady step and unflinching courage. Nor is it a course likely to be altered by threatenings, come from what quarter or whatever interest they may.

✳

The Independent

FEBRUARY 8, 1866

Mr. Frederick Douglass drew the largest house of the season at the Brooklyn Academy of Music, last [Monday] evening, to hear his lecture on "The Assassination and Its Lessons." Unusual interest had been awakened in Douglass, before his coming, in view of the fact that the Academy of Music had first been refused to him on account of his color. But at last, a vote of the directors stood 11 to 5 in favor of granting the platform. Of course, after such an attempt against free speech, the most intelligent audience which it is possible to gather in that city saluted the orator with a welcome refreshing to witness and delightful to remember. The speech was strong, high-toned and noble; abounding in characteristic passages of argument, humor, and satire; making, on the whole, a masterly performance, and an impressive occasion. We understand the names of the five dissenting directors are to be written on shells and deposited in the Brooklyn Historical Society's collection of Long Island fossils.

—Theodore Tilton

CHAPTER 6

SOURCES OF DANGER TO THE REPUBLIC

Plymouth Church
December 1866

I n early September 1866, Douglass and Tilton caused
a stir at a convention of Republicans in Philadelphia.
Thaddeus Stevens had discouraged Douglass from
attending the event, fearing that his presence could
undermine white support for Radical Republican candi-
dates in the upcoming midterm elections. Tilton, meanwhile, publicly supported Douglass's participation, and
Republicans in Rochester concurred, voting to send the
hometown figure to the event.

To the consternation of Stevens and others, Douglass and Tilton chose to make a grand statement—by
walking together arm in arm in the opening procession to Independence Hall. To Douglass's surprise,
the gesture was cheered on by Philadelphians, both
black and white. Later that same day, he would speak

on behalf of black voting rights at the convention.[86]

Back in Brooklyn, the *Eagle*'s Thomas Kinsella took issue with such a dramatic display of interracial unity.

✴

THE BROOKLYN DAILY EAGLE

TUESDAY EVENING, 4 SEPTEMBER 1866

"PAR NOBILE FRATRUM"

The devoted attachment of Damon and Pythias[87] has found a parallel in Fred. Douglass and Theodore Tilton. They are not only seen arm-in-arm whenever they meet, but they cannot open their mouths without singing each other's praise. Theodore calls Frederick "my friend Douglass." Frederick gushingly told Tilton he was the "whitest Negro of his acquaintance," and Tilton was so proud of the title that he adopted it. The expression is not quite as happy as that of the old darkey preacher who wanted to compliment a white man who had been friendly to his race—"Bless dat man, he got a white face, but he hab a black heart." But the assorted twins have turned up in the Philadelphia Mulatto Convention, and have been

---

86 Stevens's cautious position was atypical, and he remained on close terms with many black leaders (and Douglass's son, Charles, would attend his funeral procession in August 1868). For a description of the Philadelphia event, see McFeely, *Frederick Douglass*, 250–252.

87 Greek myth of two friends who plot to kill the king Dionysius, who becomes so impressed by the pair's willingness to sacrifice for one another that he spares both.

playing their usual roles with much éclat. The arm-in-arm act brought down the house, though some of the audience were too dull to see the sentiment of the thing. Like the stupid people at the theatre who laugh at the pathetic scene of a play, they thought Tilton and Douglass were trying to burlesque the South Carolina-Massachusetts feature of the original Philadelphia convention,[88] and were moved to mirth instead of tears at the touching spectacle.

This was not unnatural as the whole affair is looked upon as a clumsy parody of the great National Union Convention. The second scene of the new version of Damon and Pythias was in the selection of officers of the Northern section of the convention—for this "Union" convention is divided into Northern and Southern sections. Fred. Douglass was on the list of vice-presidents. When his name was read he got up and resigned in favor of his friend Tilton. This is quite touching, but it is a bad stroke of policy. As Douglass is the only colored man in the convention, and he has got more brains than all the white trash in the party, he ought to have a prominent position. This convention goes in for elevating the Negroes to equality with white men in all things. They should give a practical proof of it to convince the darkies of their sincerity. Tilton may be a good enough

---

88 A few weeks prior to the Republican gathering, Philadelphia had hosted a meeting of pro-Johnson National Union forces. There, South Carolina's Governor James Orr had strode arm in arm with former Union General Daniel Sickles, in a display of North-South unity. See McFeely, *Frederick Douglass*, 251.

Negro in his own estimation, and Douglas may, in the excess of friendship, give up his position to Tilton, but the shrewd darkies will not see it in that light. They have not much confidence in cream-colored niggers, and will not accept a thoroughly bleached specimen like Tilton. The convention has made a mistake in letting Fred resign.

❉

Throughout 1866, President Johnson continued to display clear hostility toward black equality, most dramatically by vetoing a Civil Rights bill and opposing passage of the Fourteenth Amendment. Such positions caused him to lose some of the earlier support he had received from leading Republicans. In the wake of the BAM controversy, Beecher had spoken in favor of black suffrage, and he distanced himself from Johnson. At the same time, Beecher and Douglass patched up their relationship. On Monday, December 17, 1866, Douglass came to Plymouth Church, where he delivered a new speech, "Sources of Danger to the Republic," which he had debuted in Hoboken two days earlier.[89] In it, Douglass submitted a forceful critique of what he viewed as structural flaws in the US political system, particularly

---

89 On Saturday, December 15, Douglass spoke at Odd Fellows' Hall in Hoboken, New Jersey. According to the *New York Herald* (December 16, 1866), "The attendance was very slim, but very attentive and enthusiastic at some of the more radical points of the lecture."

pertaining to various powers of the executive branch. Many of his criticisms—of the veto power, the role of the vice president, etc.—stemmed directly from his view of Johnson.

The *Eagle* reported that there was "good attendance" at Plymouth, while the *Herald* noted that the audience contained "a slight sprinkling of colored faces, the lecturer never failing to excite special interest among those of his own race." One example of a white attendee's enthusiastic response would prompt a snide editorial from Thomas Kinsella, which follows the speech below. Citing reasons of space, the *Eagle* only published "extracts" of the lecture. Thus, here is a complete version of the speech, which Douglass delivered in St. Louis in early February of 1867, with audience responses from the *Eagle* account in italics.[90]

❋

"Sources of Danger to the Republic"

Ladies and Gentlemen: I know of no greater misfortunes to individuals than an over-confidence in their

90 See *Brooklyn Eagle* (December 18, 1866), *New York Herald* (December 18, 1866), and *Daily Missouri Democrat* (February 8, 1867). According to the *Herald*, Douglass was "rather tardy, [arriving] considerably after eight o'clock." But the audience "listened with close attention, and as the dusky orator easily and fluently warmed into occasional passages of fervid eloquence, he was greeted with decided plaudits of appreciation and endorsement."

own perfections, and I know of fewer misfortunes that can happen to a nation greater than an over-confidence in the perfection of its government. It is common on great occasions to hear men speak of our republican form of government as a model of surpassing excellence—the best government on earth, a masterpiece of statesmanship—and destined at some period not very remote to supercede all other forms of government among men; and when our patriotic orators would appear in some degree recondite as well as patriotic, they treat us to masterly disquisitions upon what they are pleased to term "the admirable mechanism of our Constitution." They discourse wisely of its checks and balances, and the judicious distribution of the various powers.

I am certainly not here this evening rudely to call in question these very pleasing assumptions of governmental superiority on our part; they are perfectly natural; they are consistent with our natural self-love and our national pride; and when they are not employed, as they too often are, in the bad service of a blind, unreasoning, stubborn conservatism, to shelter old-time abuses and discourage manly criticism, and to defeat needed measures of amendment, they are comparatively harmless, though we may not always be able to assent to the good taste with which they are urged. It is well enough, however, once in a while to remind Americans that they are not alone in this species of self-laudation; that in fact there are many men, reputed wise and good men, living in other parts of the planet, under other forms of government, aristocratic, autocratic, oligarchic, and monarchical, who are just as confident of the good qualities of their government as we are of our own. It is true, also, that many good men, at home and abroad, and especially abroad, looking upon our republican experiment from afar, in the cool, calm light of their philosophy, have already discovered, or think that they have discovered, a decline or decay, and the certain downfall of our republican institutions, and the speedy substitution of some other form of government for our democratic institutions.

Those who entertain these opinions of our government are not entirely without reason, plausible reason, in support of it. The fact that the ballot box, upon which we have relied so long as the chief source of strength, is the safety valve of our institutions through which the explosive passions of the populace could pass off harmlessly, has failed us—broken down under us, and that a formidable rebellion has arisen, the minority of the people in one section of the country united, animated and controlled by a powerful sectional interest, have rebelled, and for four long years disputed the authority of the constitutional majority of the people, is regarded as a telling argument against the prevailing assumption of our national stability and the impregnability of our institutions. Besides, they point us, and very decidedly, to the fact that there seemed to be no adequate comprehension of the character of this rebellion at the beginning of it, and seemed also to be nothing like a proper spirit of enthusiasm manifested by the people in support of the government. They point us to the tardiness and hesitation and doubt, and the disposition to yield up the government to the arrogant demands of conspirators; and they profess themselves now able to see the same want of spirit, manliness and courage in the matter of reconstruction since the rebellion has been suppressed. They point us also to the fact that so far as the government is concerned, there must be either an indisposition or an inability either to punish traitors or to reward and protect loyal men; and they say, very wisely, as I think, that a nation that cannot hate treason cannot love loyalty.

They point us also to the fact that there are growing antagonisms, forces bitter and unrelenting between the different branches of our government—the executive against the legislative, and the judicial in some instances against both. They point us also to the obvious want of gratitude on the part of the nation, its disposition to sacrifice its best friends and to make peace with its bitterest enemies; the fact that it has placed its only true allies under the political heels of the very men who with broad blades and bloody hands sought the destruction of the republic. They point us to the fact that loyal men by the score, by the hundred, have been deliberately and outrageously, and in open daylight, slaughtered by the known enemies of the country, and thus far that the murderers are at large: unquestioned by the law, unpunished by justice, unrebuked even by the public opinion of the localities where the crimes were committed. Under the whole heavens you cannot find any government besides our own [that is so] indifferent to the lives of its loyal subjects. They tell us, moreover, that the lives of republics have been short, stormy, and saddening to the hopes of the friends of freedom, and they tell us, too, that ours will prove no exception to this general rule.

Now, why have I referred to these unfavorable judgments of American institutions? Not, certainly, to endorse them; neither to combat them; but as offering a reason why the Americans should take a little less extravagant view of the excellencies of our institutions. We should scrutinize them a little more closely and weigh their value a little more impartially than we are accustomed to do. We ought to examine our government, and I am here tonight, and I rejoice that in [Brooklyn] that there is liberty enough, civilization enough, to tolerate free inquiry at this point as well as any other. I am here tonight in a little different capacity from what I ordinarily am, or what I have been before the American people. In other days—darker days than these—I appeared before the American people simply as a member of a despised, outraged and downtrodden race; simply to plead that the chains of the bondmen be broken; simply to plead that the auction block shall no more be in use for the sale of human flesh. I appear here no longer as a whipped, scarred slave—no longer as the advocate merely of an enslaved race, but in the high and commanding character of an American citizen, having the interest that every true citizen should have in the welfare, the stability, the permanence and the prosperity of our free institutions, and in this spirit I shall criticize our government tonight.

Now, while I discard all Fourth of July extravagances about the Constitution, and about its framers, even I can speak respectfully of that instrument and respectfully of the men who framed it. To be sure my early condition in life was not very favorable to the growth of what men call patriotism and reverence for institutions— certainly not for the "peculiar institution" from which I graduated [*laughter*]—yet even I can speak respectfully of the Constitution. For one thing I feel grateful—at least I think the fathers deserve homage of mankind for this—that against the assumptions, against the inducements to do otherwise, they have given us a Constitution commensurate in its beneficent arrangements with the wants of common humanity; that it embraces man as man. There is nothing in it of a narrow description. They could establish a Constitution free from bigotry, free from superstition, free from sectarian prejudices, caste or political distinction.[91]

In the eye of that great instrument we are neither

---

91 For a discussion of Douglass's view of the Constitution, see footnote 43 above.

Jews, Greeks, Barbarians or Cythians, but fellow-citizens of a common country, embracing all men of all colors. The fathers of this republic did not learn to insert the word *white,* or to determine men's rights by their color. They did not base their legislation upon the differences among men in the length of their noses or the twist of their hair, but upon the broad fact of a common human nature.

I doubt if at any time during the last fifty years we could have received a Constitution so liberal from the sons as we have received from the fathers of [this] republic. They were above going down, as certain men—Caucasian and Teutonic ethnologists—have recently done, on their knees and measuring the human heel to ascertain the amount of intelligence he should have. They were above that. That is a modern improvement or invention.

Some have undertaken to prove the identity of the Negro, or the relationship of the Negro with the monkey from the length of his heel, forgetting what is the fact, that the monkey has no heel at all, and that in fact the longer a man's heel is the further he is from the monkey. Our fathers did not fall into this mistake. They made a constitution for men, not for color, not for features. In the eye of that great instrument the moment the chains are struck from the limbs of the humblest and most whip-scarred slave he may rise to any position for which his talents and character fit him For this I say the fathers are entitled to the profound gratitude of mankind—that against all temptations to do otherwise, they have given us a liberal constitution. [*Applause.*]

But wise and good as that instrument is, at this point and at many others, it is simply a human contrivance. It is the work of man and men struggling with many of the prejudices and infirmities common to man, and it is not strange that we should find in their constitution some evidences of their infirmity and prejudices. Time and experience and the ever-increasing light of reason are constantly making manifest those defects and those imperfections. It is for us, living eighty years after them, and therefore eighty years wiser than they, to remove those defects—to improve the character of our constitution at this point where we find those defects. [*Applause.*]

I was rather glad at one feature in the effect produced by the rebellion. It for a time depressed the national exultation over the perfection of the Constitution of the United States. The uprising of that rebellion was a severe blow to our national extravagance at this point, but the manner in which we have met the rebellion, and as soon as we have succeeded in suppressing it, conquering the rebels and scattering their military forces, our old-time notions of our perfect system of government have revived, and there is an indisposition on the part of some men to entertain propositions for amending the Constitution. But I think that a right view of our trouble, instead of increasing our confidence in the perfection of the fundamental structure of the government, ought to do quite the reverse; it ought to impress us with the sense of our national insecurity by disclosing, as it does disclose, the slenderness of the thread on which the national life was suspended, and showing us how small a circumstance might have whelmed our government in the measureless abyss of ruin, prepared for it by the rebels.

We succeeded in putting down the rebellion. And wherein is the secret of that success? Not in, I think, the superior structure of our government, by any means. We succeeded in that great contest because, during at least the latter part of the war, the loyal armies fought on the side of human nature; fought on the side of justice, civil order and liberty. This rebellion was struck with death the instant Abraham Lincoln inscribed on our banner the word "Emancipation." Our armies went up to battle thereafter for the best aspirations of the human soul in every quarter of the globe, and we conquered. The rebel armies fought well, fought bravely, fought desperately, but they fought in fetters. Invisible chains were about them. Deep down in their own consciences there was an accusing voice reminding them that they were fighting for chains and slavery, and not for freedom. They were in chains—entangled with the chains of their own slaves. They not only struggled with our gigantic armies, and with the skill of our veteran generals, but they fought against the moral sense of the

nineteenth century. They fought against their own better selves—they fought against the good in their own
souls. They were weakened thereby; their weakness was
our strength, hence our success. And our success over
the rebels is due to another cause quite apart from the
perfection of our structure of government. It is largely
owing to the fact that the nation happened—for it only
happened—we happened to have in the presidential
chair, an honest man.

It might have been otherwise. It was our exceeding
good fortune that Abraham Lincoln—not William H.
Seward—received the nomination at Chicago in 1860.
Had Seward—judging him by his present position[92]—or
Franklin Pierce, or Millard Fillmore, or James Buchanan,
or had that other embodiment of political treachery,
meanness, baseness, ingratitude, the vilest of the vile,
the basest of the base, the most execrable of the execrable of modern times—he who shall be nameless—
occupied the presidential chair, your magnificent republic might have been numbered with the things that were.

We talk about the power of the people over this government, of its admirable checks and balances, its wisely

92 In 1860, William Seward, a former governor and senator from New York, had
led on the first two ballots at the party convention in Chicago, before Lincoln took
the nomination on the third. Seward then served as Lincoln's secretary of state, and
successfully kept the British and French from allying with the Confederacy. He also
helped push through passage of the Thirteenth Amendment. But after he stayed on
as secretary of state under Johnson, Seward supported the president's reconciliation
with the South, which did not include black suffrage. See Blassingame and
McKivigan, eds., *The Frederick Douglass Papers*, Series 1, Vol. 4, 155.

arranged machinery; but remember those three months, the last three months of Buchanan's administration. It is impossible to think wisely and deeply without learning a lesson of the inherent weakness of our republican structure. For three long months the nation saw their army and their navy scattered and the munitions of war of the government placed in the hands of its enemies.[93] The people could do nothing but bite their lips in silent agony. They were on a mighty stream afloat, with all their liberties at stake and a faithless pilot on their boat. They could not help this. They were in a current which they could neither resist nor control. In the rapids of a political Niagara, the nation [was swept] on in silent agony toward the awful cataract in the distance to receive it. Our power was unable to stay the treachery.

We appealed, to be sure—we pointed out through our principles the right way—but we were powerless, and we saw no help till the man, Lincoln, appeared in the theater of action and extended his honest hand to save the republic. No, we owe nothing to our form of government for our preservation as a nation, nothing whatever; nothing to its checks, nor to its balances, nor to its wise division of powers and duties. It was an honest president backed up by intelligent and loyal people—high-minded

---

93 Buchanan was widely seen as unprepared to deal with the secession crisis that began in December 1860. Among other problems, federal munition and naval supplies were largely stored in Southern states, meaning Confederate forces controlled them. *Ibid.*, 155–56.

men that constitute the state—who regarded society as superior to its forms, the spirit as above the letter. Men as more than country, and as superior to the Constitution. They resolved to save the country with the Constitution if they could, but at any rate to save the country. To this we owe our present safety as a nation.

[That] a defective ship with a skillful captain, a hard-handed and honest crew, may manage to weather a considerable storm is no proof that our old bark is sound in all her planks, bolts and timbers. [It is only] by constant pumping and extraordinary exertions that we have managed to keep afloat and at last reach the shore.

I propose to speak to you of the sources of danger to our republic. These may be described under two heads, those which are esoteric in their character and those which are exoteric. I shall discourse of these in the order now stated. Let it not, however, be supposed by my intelligent audience that I concede anything to those who hold to the inherent weakness of a republican form of government. Far from this. The points of weakness in our government don't touch its republican character. On the contrary I hold that a republican form of government is the strongest government on earth when it is thoroughly republican. Our republican government is weak only as it touches or partakes of the character of monarchy or an aristocracy or an oligarchy. In its republican features it is strong. In its despotic features it is weak. Our government, in its ideas, is a government of the people. But unhappily it was framed under conditions unfavorable to purely republican results, it was projected and completed under the influence of institutions quite unfavorable to a pure republican form of government—slavery on the one hand, monarchy on the other.

Late in a man's life his surroundings exert but a limited influence upon him—they are usually shaken off; but only a hero may shake off the influences of birth and early surroundings; the champion falls—the cause remains. Such is the constitution of the human mind, that there can be no such thing as immediate emancipation, either from slavery or from monarchy. An instant is sufficient to snap the chains; a century is not too much to obliterate all traces of former bondage.

It was easy for the fathers of the republic, comparatively so at least, to drive the red-coats from our continent, but it was not easy to drive the ideas and associations that surrounded the British throne and emanated from the monarch of this country. Born, as the fathers of this republic were, under monarchical institutions, they were disposed to blend something of the old error with the new truth, or of the newly discovered truth of liberty asserted in the Declaration of Independence. The eclectic principle may work pretty well in some governments, but it does not work well in our government. Here there must be unity; unity of idea; unity of object and accord of motive as well as of principles in order to [attain] a harmonious, happy and prosperous result.

The idea of putting new wine into old bottles or mending old garments with new cloth was not peculiar to the Jew[94]; it came down to the fathers, and it is showing itself now amongst us. We are disposed to assent to the abolition of slavery, but we wish to retain something of slavery in the new dispensation. We are willing that the chains of the slave shall be broken if a few links can be left on his arm or on his leg. Your fathers were in some respects after the same pattern. They gave us a Constitution made in the shadow of slavery and of monarchy, and in its character it partakes in some of its features of both those unfavorable influences. Now, as I have said, I concede nothing to those who hold to the inherent weakness of our government or a republican form of government. The points of weakness or the features that weaken our government are exotic. They have been incorporated and interposited from other forms of government, and it is the business of this day and this generation to purge them from the Constitution.

In fact, I am here tonight as a democrat, a genuine democrat dyed in the wool. [*Laughter*.] I am here to advocate a genuine democratic republic; to make this a republican form of government, purely a republic, a genuine republic; free it from everything that looks to-

---

94 From Matthew 9:16–17.

ward monarchy; eliminate all foreign elements, [and] all alien elements from it. [I aim to] blot out from it everything antagonistic of republicanism declared by the fathers, whose idea was that all governments derived their first powers from the consent of the governed; [to] make it a government of the people, by the people and for the people, and for all the people, each for all and all for each. [I aim to] blot out all discriminations against any person, theoretically or practically, to keep no man from the ballot box or jury box or the cartridge box because of his color—[and to] exclude no woman from the ballot box because of her sex. [*Applause.*] Let the government of the country rest securely down upon the shoulders of the whole nation; let there be no shoulder that does not bear up its proportion of the burdens of the government. Let there be no conscience, no intellect in the land not directly responsible for the moral character of the government—for the honor of the government. Let it be a genuine republic, in which every man subject to it is represented in it, and I see no reason why a republic may not stand and flourish while the world stands. [*Renewed applause.*]

Now, the first source of weakness to a republican government is the one-man power. I rejoice that we are at last startled into a consciousness of the existence of this one-man power. If it was necessary for Jefferson Davis and his peculiar friends to resort to arms in order to show the danger of tolerating the slave power in our government, we are under great obligations to Andrew Johnson for disclosing to us the unwisdom of tolerating the one-man power in their government. And if now we shall be moved, as I hope we shall, to revise our Constitution so as to entirely free it from the one-man power, to curtail or abridge that power, and reduce it to a manageable point, his accidental occupancy of the presidential chair will not be the unmitigated calamity we have been accustomed to regard it. It will be a blessing in disguise though pretty heavily disguised. For disguise it as we will, this one-man power is in our constitution. It has its sheet anchor firmly in the soil of our constitution. Mr. Johnson has sometimes overstepped this power, in certain conditions of his mind, which are quite frequent, and mistaken himself for the United States instead of the president of the United States. The fault is not entirely due to his marvelous vanity, but to the constitution under which he lives. It is there in that Constitution.

It is true that our president is not our king for life; he is here only temporarily. I say king [because] Mr. Seward, you know, took it upon himself to introduce Andrew Johnson to the simple-hearted people of Michigan as king. "Will you have him as your president or as your king," said the astute secretary of state, evidently regarding the one title as appropriate to Andy Johnson as the other.[95] There is a good deal of truth in it, for in

95 According to Blassingame and McKivigan (p. 159), when Seward made these comments (in early September 1866), he was actually distinguishing between the

fact he is invested with kingly power, with an arbitrariness equal to any crown-head in Europe. Despite our boasts of the power of the people, your president can rule you as with a rod of iron. It is true he is only elected for four years—he is only a four-year-old—and the brief time of the term would seem to be a security against misbehavior. [It is] a security and a guarantee of good conduct, for the most turbulent of men, [who] can manage to behave themselves for short periods—always excepting the "Humble Individual."[96] But this brief time is no security, [as] to my mind it furnishes impunity rather than security. We bear, in one of these presidents' behavior, arrogance and arbitrariness that we would not bear with but for the limited term of his service. We would not bear it an hour—the disgrace and scandal that we now stagger under—did we not know that two short, silent years will put an end to our misery in this respect.

Well, we do choose him; we elect him, and we are free while we are electing him. [As a] slave, when I was first given the privilege hereafter of choosing my own master at the end of the year, I was very much delighted. It struck me as a large concession to my manhood, the idea that I had the right to choose a master at the end of the year, and if I was kicked, and cuffed, bruised and beaten during the year, it was some satisfaction to

two titles, encouraging the audience to view Johnson as the president, not a king.
96 Johnson's proclivity for talking about himself led the Republican press to cast him in sarcastic terms. *Ibid.*, 160.

know that after all, old fellow, I will shake you off at the end of the year. I thought it a great thing to be able to choose my own master. I was quite intoxicated with this little bit of liberty—and I would dance from Christmas to New Year on the strength of it. But, as I grew older and a trifle wiser, I began to be dissatisfied with this liberty, the liberty of choosing another master. I found that what I wanted, that what I needed, what was essential to my manhood was not another master, not a new master, not an old master, but the right to the power under the law to be my own master.

From this little bit of experience—slave experience—I have elaborated quite a lengthy chapter of political philosophy, applicable to the American people. You are free to choose, but after you have chosen your freedom is gone, just as mine was—gone, and our power is gone to a large extent under the framework of our government when you have chosen. You are free to choose, free while you are voting, free while you are dropping a piece of paper into the box with some names on it—I won't tell how those names got on it, [for] that would evince, perhaps, a culpable familiarity with politics to do that. But you are free while you are dropping in your vote—going, going, gone. When your president is elected, once familiarly seated in the national saddle, his feet in the stirrups, his hand on the reins, he can drive the national animal almost where he will. He can administer this government with a contempt for public opinion, for the opinions and wishes of the people, such as no crowned head in Europe imitates towards his subjects . . .

Now what are the elements that enter into this one-man power and swell it to the formidable measure at which we find it at this time? The first thing is the immense patronage of the President of the United States—the patronage of money, of honor, of place and power. He is able to divide among his friends and among his satellites—attaching men to his person and to his political fortunes—a hundred million of dollars per annum in time of peace, and uncounted thousands of millions of dollars in time of war are virtually at his disposal. This is an influence which can neither be weighed, measured nor otherwise estimated. The very thought of it is overwhelming. This amount of money lodged outside of the government in unfriendly hands could be made a formidable lever for the destruction of the government. It is a direct assault upon the national virtue. While the President of the United States can exalt whom he will, cast down whom he will; he can place A into office for agreeing with him in opinion, and cause B to be put out of office because of an honest difference of opinion with him. Who does not see that the tendency to agreement will be a million times stronger than the tendency to differ, even though truth should be in favor of difference. From this power—this patronage—has arisen the popular political maxim that "to the victors belong the spoils," and that other vulgar expression of the same idea by Postmaster General Randall that no man shall eat the president's "bread and butter" who does not endorse the president's "policy." The first thing that an American is taught at the cradle side is never to fight against his bread and butter . . .[97]

Another source of evil in the one-man power is the veto power. I am in favor of abolishing the veto power completely. It has no business in our Constitution. It is alien to every idea of republican government—borrowed from the old world, from king craft and priest craft, and all other adverse craft to republican government. It is antirepublican, antidemocratic, anti–common sense. It is based upon the idea, the absurdity, that one man is more than many men—that one man separate from the people by his exalted station, sitting apart from the people in his room, surrounded by his friends, his cliques, his satellites, will be likely to bring to the consideration of public measures, a higher wisdom, a larger knowledge, a purer patriotism, than will the representatives of the republic. [Congressmen are] in the face and in the presence of the multitude, with the flaming sword of the press waving over them, directly responsible to their constituents, immediately in communication with the great heart of the people—[but the veto means] that one man will be likely to govern more wisely than will a majority of the people. It is borrowed from the old world; it is alien to our in-

---

97 Douglass then calls for Congress, not the president, to control the patronage process.

stitutions; it is opposed to the very genius of free institutions, and I want to see it struck out of our Constitution. I believe that two heads are better than one, and I shall not stultify myself by saying that one head, even though it be the head of Andrew Johnson, is more than almost two-thirds of the representatives of the American people. *We have a veto for breakfast every morning!*[98] Is that republicanism? Is that democracy? Is that consistent with the idea that the people shall rule? I think not.

I believe majorities can be despotic and have been arbitrary, but arbitrary to whom? Arbitrary when arbitrary at all, always to unrepresented classes. What is the remedy? A consistent republic in which there shall be no unrepresented classes. For when all classes are represented the rights of all classes will be respected. It is a remarkable fact, and we Americans may well ponder it, that although the veto is entirely consistent with monarchical government and entirely inconsistent with republican government, the government of England, which is a monarchy, has not exercised the veto power once in 150 years. There where it is consistent it is never used. Here where it is inconsistent, and at war with the genius of our institutions, we can have a little veto every morning. Where the people rule they are the vetoed. When

---

98 In late February 1866, Johnson vetoed the Freedmen's Bureau Bill, thus undermining federal action on behalf of blacks in Southern states; in late March, he vetoed the Civil Rights Bill, which laid the groundwork for the Fourteenth Amendment, ensuring black equality; and in July, he vetoed a second version of the Freedmen's Bureau Bill. Congress overrode the latter two vetoes.

any measure passes the House of Commons or House of Lords, it is sure of the royal assent. Popular as Queen Victoria is, honored as she is queen, loved as she is a mother, as a good citizen of the realm, it would cost her the crown to veto a measure passed by the people's representatives in the House of Commons and by the House of Lords. And if in a monarchy the representatives of the people can be trusted to govern themselves without the veto, republican Americans, can't you? Have done with that veto. It is a fruitful source of mischief, and bad bold men. A man of vigorous intellect, imperious will, fiery temper and boundless ambition finds in that veto a convenient instrument for the gratification of all his desires and his base ambition. Do away with it, blot it out from your government, and you will have done with the antagonism between the legislative arm and the executive arm of the government. Make your president what you ought to be, not more than he ought to be, and you should see to it that such changes should be made in the Constitution of the United States that your president is simply your executive, that he is there not to make laws, but to enforce them; not to defy your will, but to enforce your high behests.

I would [also] abolish, if I had it in my power, the two-term principle. Away with that. While that principle remains in the Constitution[99]—while the president

---

99 As Blassingame and McKivigan note (p. 161), "George Washington established the precedent for a two-term presidency, but it was not part of the US Constitution,

can be his own successor, and is eligible to succeed himself, he will not be warm in his seat in the presidential chair (such is poor human nature) before he will begin to scheme for a second election. It is a standing temptation to him to use the powers of his office in such a manner as to promote his own political fortune. The presidency is too valuable to allow a man who occupies the position the means of perpetuating himself in that office. Another objection to this provision of the Constitution is, that we have a divided man in the presidential chair. The duties of the presidency are such as to require a whole man, the whole will, and the whole work; but the temptation of a president is to make himself a president of a presidential party as well as of the country, and the result is that we are only half served. What we want is the entire service of a man reduced to one term, and then he can bring to the service of his country an undivided man, an undivided sense of duty and devote his energies to the discharge of his office without selfish ends or aims. Blot out this two-term system.

Another thing I would abolish—the pardoning power. I should take that right out of the hands of this one man. The argument against it is in some respects similar to that used against the veto power. Those against the veto power are equally persistent against the pardoning power, and there is a good reason why we

as Douglass implies."

should do away with the pardoning power in the hands of the president, [which] is that our government may at some time be in the hands of a bad man. When in the hands of a good man it is all well enough, and we ought to have our government so shaped that even when in the hands of a bad man we shall be safe. And we know that the people are usually well-intentioned. A certain percentage are thieves, a certain percentage are robbers, murderers, assassins, blind, insane and idiots. But the great mass of men are well-intentioned, and we should watch the individual. Trust the masses always. That is good democracy, is it not? Not modern, but old-fashioned.

But my argument is this: A bad president, for instance, has the power to do what? What can he not do? If he wanted to revolutionize this government, he could easily do it with this ponderous power; it would be an auxiliary power. He could cry "havoc, and let slip the dogs of war,"[100] and say to the conspirators: "I am with you. If you succeed, all is well. If you fail, I will interpose the shield of my pardon, and you are safe. If your property is taken away from you by Congress, I will pardon and restore your property. Go on and revolutionize the government; I will stand by you." The bad man will say or might say this. I am not sure but we have got a man now who comes very near saying it. Let us have done with this pardoning power. We have had enough of this.

---

100 A line from *Julius Caesar*.

Pardoning! How inexpressibly base have been the uses made by this power—this beneficent power. It has been that with which a treacherous president has trafficked. He has made it the means of securing adherents to himself instead of securing allegiance to the government. Let us have done with closet pardons—pardons obtained by bad men; pardons obtained by questionable women; pardons obtained in the most disgraceful and scandalous manner. Drive this pardoning power out of the government and put it in the legislative arm of the government in some way. Let a committee of the House of Representatives and Senate of the United States determine who shall be the recipients of the clemency at the hands of the nation. Let it not come from an individual, but let it come from the people. An outraged people know to whom to extend this clemency.

Another thing I am in favor of [is] abolishing the office of the vice president. Let us have no more vice presidents. We have had bad luck with them. We don't need them. There is no more need of electing a vice president at the same time we elect a president than there is need of electing a second wife when we have got one already. "Sufficient unto the day is the evil thereof."[101] The argument against the vice presidency is to me very conclusive. It may be briefly stated thus: The presidency of the United States, like the crown of a monarchy, is a

101 From Matthew 6:34.

tempting bauble. It is a very desirable thing. Men are men. Ambition is ambition the world over. History is constantly repeating itself. There is not a single crown in Europe that has not [at] some time been stained with innocent blood—not one. For the crown, men have murdered their friends who have dined at the table with them; for the crown, men have sent the assassin to the cells of their own brothers and their own sisters, and plunged the dagger into their own warm, red blood. For the crown all manner of crimes have been committed.

The presidency is equally a tempting bauble in this country. I am not for placing that temptation so near any man as it is placed when we elect a vice president. I am not for electing a man to the presidential chair, and then putting a man behind him with his ambition all leading that way—with his desires, his thoughts, all directed upon that chair, with a knowledge, at the same time, that only the president's life stands between him and the object of his ambition. I am not for placing a man behind the president, within striking distance of him, whose interest, whose ambition, whose every inclination is to be served by his getting that chair.

The wall of assassination is too thin to be placed between a man and the presidency of the United States. Let your vice president be unknown to himself and unknown to the people. Let him be in the mass till there is need for him. Don't plump him right upon the president. Your president is unsafe while the shadow of the vice president falls upon the presidential chair. How easy it would be to procure [the] death of any man where there are such temptations as that offered. A clique, a clan, a ring, usually forms about the vice president.

The president dies, and in steps the vice president. He is reminded at once of his old pledges, and he begins to try to redeem them by turning against the party who elected him. It is a remarkable fact that in no instance has any vice president followed out the policy of the president that he was elected with. Elected on the same ticket, on the same platform, at the same time, at the instant the president is taken off the vice president has reversed the machinery of the policy on which he was elected in every instance. [William Henry] Harrison was the first man suspected of entertaining opinions unfavorable to slavery. He died in a month. He was succeeded by whom? By John Tyler, one of the most violent propagandists of slavery that ever trod this continent. Where was the Whig party that elected him? Nowhere. Where was the policy on which he was elected? Nowhere.

[Zachary] Taylor, though a slaveholding man and an honest man towards his constituents and the people of the country, the moment it was ascertained he was in favor of admitting California as a free state if she saw fit to come with a constitution of that character and was opposed to paying ten millions of dollars to Texas on account of the claim on New Mexico, there were means at hand to kill him. He died and was followed by whom? By a vile sycophant who spit on the policy of his predecessor, and put himself in the service of the very men whom that president had offended.[102] Well, they tried to murder even James Buchanan in order that he should be followed by a younger, stronger traitor than himself. They put Mr. [John C.] Breckinridge behind him [as vice president], and when he went down to Washington they carried him to the National Hotel and helped him to a large dose of poison. But in that instance the poison met its match. Who doubts that James Buchanan was poisoned? It was notorious at the time, and no doubt poisoned for a purpose.

Today we mourn, the nation has to mourn, that the nation has a president made president by the bullet of an assassin. I do not say that he knew that his noble predecessor was to be murdered. I do not say that he had any hand in it; but this I do say, without fear of contradiction, that the men who murdered Abraham Lincoln knew Andrew Johnson as we know him now. Let us have done with these vice presidents. The nation can easily call a man to fill the presidential chair in case of death; besides, he is not half so likely to die. It is a little remarkable, too, that whilst presidents die, vice presidents never die. There is nobody behind them.[103]

---

102 Millard Fillmore took office when Taylor died of dysentery in July 1850. Rumors persisted that Taylor was poisoned by proslavery sympathizers.
103 The *Eagle* noted, "In this connection, [Douglass] took to speak of impeachment. He said that Congress would not dare impeach the president. That was the plain English of it." In early 1868, the House voted to impeach Johnson but the Senate

Well, I had marked a number of points I intended to dwell upon. I am taking up perhaps too much of your time, to go further with internal sources of danger to the republic. I had purposed to have spoken specially of secret diplomacy, but I pass it over as one of the sources of weakness to our republican form of government. I may be told that in pointing out these sources of weakness that it is easy to find fault but not so easy to find remedies. I admit it, I agree that it requires more talent to build a decent pig sty than to tear down a considerable palace; and yet when the ship is to be repaired, it is of some consequence to find out where the unsound timbers are, when the opening seam is where the corroded bolt is, that we put in sounder. I have been indicating where these points of unsoundness are. And I think I can leave this matter of Reconstruction to the high constructive talent of this Anglo-Saxon race. The Negro has done his part if he succeeds in pointing out the source of danger to the republic. You will have done your part when you have corrected or removed these sources of danger. We have already grappled with very dangerous elements in our government, and we have performed a manly part, we have removed errors. There are some [more] errors to be removed, not so dangerous, not so shocking, perhaps, as those with which we have grappled; but nevertheless dangers requiring removal. Happy

did not reach the two-thirds majority to do so.

will it be for us, happy will it be for the land, happy for coming generations, if we shall discover these sources of danger, and grapple with them in time without the aid of a second rebellion—without the people being lashed and stung into another military necessity.

It is sad to think that half the glory, half the honor due to the great act of emancipation, was lost in the tardiness of its performance. It has now gone irrevocably into history—not as an act of sacred choice by a great nation, of the right as against the wrong, of truth as against falsehood, of liberty as against slavery—but as a military necessity. We are called upon to be faithful to the American government for our emancipation as black men, we do feel thankful, and we have the same reason to be thankful, that the Israelites had to be thankful to Pharaoh for their emancipation, for their liberties. It was not until judgments terrible, wide-sweeping, far-reaching and overwhelming, had smitten down this nation, that we were ready to part with our reverence for slavery, and ceased to quote Scripture in its defense. It was not until we felt the land trembling beneath our feet that we heard an accusing voice in the heart; the sky above was darkened, the wail came up from millions of hearthstones in our land. Our sons and brothers slain in battle, it was not until we saw our sons and brothers returning home mere stumps of men, armless, legless; it was not until we felt all crumbling beneath us and we saw the Star-Spangled Banner clinging to the masthead heavy with blood.

It was not until agony was manifested from a million of hearthstones in our land, and the Southern sky was darkened, that we managed to part with our reverence for slavery, and to place a musket on the shoulders of the black man. We may now do from choice, and from sacred choice, what we did by military necessity.

At the conclusion of his remarks, a large number of [Douglass's] admirers clustered round him of the platform to testify their delight in seeing and hearing him. Congratulations and hand-shaking were the order of the day. One lady testified her appreciation in the most unmistakable manner by a hearty kiss, publicly administered, which the venerable orator took without blushing.

✦

THE BROOKLYN DAILY EAGLE
TUESDAY EVENING, DECEMBER 18, 1866

Our reporter runs the risk of being accused of telling tales out of school in noticing the fact that at the close of Fred. Douglass' lecture, at Plymouth Church, last evening, a white woman, in the exuberance of her admiration for the colored orator, forced upon him a high token of appreciation, in a chaste, Platonic kiss. The reporter dryly adds that the fortunate black man received the salutation "without blushing." We presume that the blood of the spectators was equally undisturbed.

The ridiculous prejudice against color is fast giving way, but we protest in advance against any undue partiality to the colored rivals for feminine favor. How many white men, we would like to know, have been rewarded for their oratorical efforts at Plymouth Church with favors like that accorded to Douglass? Mr. Tilton's millennium—when the warm blood of the darkey will render at least tepid that of the New Englander—may be nearer than is imagined. But who was the heroic lady that last night gave so public a mark of her freedom from antiquated prejudice? Was she a married lady and was her husband by; or was she a spinster of uncertain age, and willing to do the best she could? Mr. Tilton ought to make inquiries on the subject. Surely there is a place in a historic picture for the woman who stretched out not only her hand, but offered her lips to the representative darkey. "How it smells—pah!"

CHAPTER 7

JOHN BROWN'S HEROIC CHARACTER

Clinton Street Baptist Church

May 1886

After the women's suffrage convention at BAM in 1869,[104] Douglass did not make any prominent appearances in Brooklyn over the next fifteen years. In 1872, he moved from Rochester to Washington, DC, where he would edit the *New National Era* and live until his death in 1895. During those last two decades he remained a prominent figure in Republican politics, and spoke forcefully against the rise of segregation.

One of his most popular speeches was his celebration of John Brown's life and legacy, which he delivered at the Clinton Street Baptist Church in Brooklyn Heights in May 1886.[105] Brooklyn's black population remained small (approximately 10,000, or 1.5 percent

---

104 For additional information about the suffrage convention, see footnote 32 above.
105 The church (no longer in existence) was located on Pierrepont Street at the corner of Clinton Street, across from the Brooklyn Historical Society.

of its total)—and the city was not a significant hotspot of black protest during the era. But there had been some positive changes in Brooklyn's political climate since Douglass's last public appearance, such as the election of Republican mayors, including Seth Low.[106]

Another sign that times had changed is that the *Eagle* was far more welcoming in its tone toward Douglass, as seen in the front-page headlines below.[107] Yet upon his return to Brooklyn, Douglass also encountered some notable continuity, namely in a receptive audience that, like the speaker, was getting on in years but remembered vividly the many struggles of the Civil War era. Throughout the two-hour lecture, the *Eagle* observed, "save for his long, snowy hair, Douglass [did] not betray his years. He stood erect and smiling throughout the long evening, and his voice has not lost its ring."

One thousand people filled the church, with many African Americans in the audience. General Stewart Woodford, a prominent local Republican politician who had presided over a regiment of black soldiers in

---

106 Low, a Brooklyn native, was mayor from 1881–1885, after which he became a leading Progressive Era reformer whose positions included president of Columbia University, mayor of New York City (1902–1903), and chairman of Booker T. Washington's Tuskegee Institute.

107 By the 1880s the *Eagle* and other papers had adopted the modern format of running the most important stories on the front page, rather than on pages 2 and 3. After Kinsella's death in 1884, St. Clair McKelway became the paper's editor for the next three decades; McKelway was a Democrat, but in the 1870s had helped build the *Eagle*'s national reputation by writing editorials with a bipartisan perspective. The Douglass story ran on May 18, 1886.

the Civil War, introduced Douglass. But according to the *Brooklyn Times*, the most popular member of the audience was Helen Pitts Douglass, Frederick's second wife. Mrs. Douglass "is not a colored woman," the paper noted, and she "received marked attention at the close of the lecture."[108]

Though he had delivered his talk about Brown many times before, Douglass still worked up a passion when describing the work of his good friend. He also displayed his talents for a type of writing he's not typically associated with—namely biography, in the poetic mold later associated with Carl Sandburg. What follows here is the text of the speech, with wording from the *Eagle*'s version included in italics.

❋

THE BROOKLYN DAILY EAGLE

MAY 18, 1886

JOHN BROWN.
Fred Douglass' Account of the Anti-Slavery Chief.

An Oft-Told Story Repeated by a Great Actor in the Struggle for Freedom—A Life of Ease Exchanged for One of Toil and Suffering—The Times Demanded the Man and He Came at the Call.

Not to fan the flame of sectional animosity now happily in the process of rapid and I hope permanent extinc-

---

108 *Brooklyn Times*, May 18, 1886.

tion, not to revive and keep alive a sense of shame and remorse for a great national crime, which has brought its own punishment, in loss of treasure, tears and blood, not to recount the long list of wrongs, inflicted on my race during more than two hundred years of merciless bondage; nor yet to draw, from the labyrinths of far-off centuries, incidents and achievements wherewith to rouse your passions, and enkindle your enthusiasm, but to pay a just debt long due, to vindicate in some degree a great historical character, of our own time and country, one with whom I was myself well acquainted, and whose friendship and confidence it was my good fortune to share, and to give you such recollections, impressions and facts, as I can, of a grand, brave and good old man, and especially to promote a better understanding of the raid upon Harpers Ferry of which he was the chief, is the object of this address.

In all the thirty years' conflict with slavery, if we except the late tremendous war, there is no subject which in its interest and importance will be remembered longer, or will form a more thrilling chapter in American history than this strange, wild, bloody and mournful drama. The story of it is still fresh in the minds of many who now hear me, but for the sake of those who may have forgotten its details, and in order to have our subject in its entire range more fully and clearly before us at the outset, I will briefly state the facts in that extraordinary transaction.

On the night of the 16th of October, 1859, there appeared near the confluence of the Potomac and Shenandoah rivers, a party of nineteen men—fourteen white and five colored. They were not only armed themselves, but had brought with them a large supply of arms for such persons as might join them. These men invaded Harpers Ferry, disarmed the watchman, took possession of the arsenal, rifle factory, armory and other government property at that place, arrested and made prisoners nearly all the prominent citizens of the neighborhood, collected about fifty slaves, put bayonets into the hands of such as were able and willing to fight for their liberty, killed three men, proclaimed general emancipation, held the ground more than thirty hours, were subsequently overpowered and nearly all killed, wounded or captured, by a body of United States troops, under command of Colonel Robert E. Lee, since famous as the rebel Gen. Lee. Three out of the nineteen invaders were captured whilst fighting, and one of these was Captain John Brown, the man who originated, planned and commanded the expedition.

At the time of his capture Capt. Brown was supposed to be mortally wounded, as he had several ugly gashes and bayonet wounds on his head and body; and apprehending that he might speedily die, or that he might be rescued by his friends, and thus the opportunity of making him a signal example of slave-holding vengeance would be lost, his captors hurried him to Charlestown two miles further within the border of Virginia, placed him in prison strongly guarded by troops, and before his wounds were healed he was brought into court, subjected to a nominal trial, convicted of high treason and inciting slaves to insurrection, and was executed. His corpse was given to his woe-stricken widow, and she, assisted by anti-slavery friends,[109] caused it to be borne to North Elba, Essex County, NY, and there his dust now reposes, amid the silent, solemn and snowy grandeur of the Adirondacks.

Such is the story; with no lines softened or hardened to my inclining. It certainly is not a story to please, but to pain. It is not a story to increase our sense of social safety and security, but to fill the imagination with wild and troubled fancies of doubt and danger. It was a sudden and startling surprise to the people of Harpers Ferry, and it is not easy to conceive of a situation more abundant in all the elements of horror and consternation.

Every feeling of the human heart was naturally outraged at this occurrence, and hence at the moment the air was full of denunciation and execration. So intense was this feeling that few ventured to whisper a word of apology. But happily reason has her voice as well as feeling, and though slower in deciding, her judgments are broader, deeper, clearer and more enduring. It is not

---

109 Theodore Tilton played an instrumental role in helping transport Brown's body through New York City. See John Strausbaugh, *City of Sedition: The History of New York City During the Civil War* (New York: Twelve, 2016), 115.

easy to reconcile human feeling to the shedding of blood for any purpose, unless indeed in the excitement which the shedding of blood itself occasions. The knife is to feeling always an offence. Even when in the hands of a skillful surgeon, it refuses consent to the operation long after reason has demonstrated its necessity. It even pleads the cause of the known murderer on the day of his execution, and calls society half-criminal when, in cold blood, it takes life as a protection of itself from crime. Let no word be said against this holy feeling; more than to law and government are we indebted to this tender sentiment of regard for human life for the safety with which we walk the streets by day and sleep secure in our beds at night. It is nature's grand police, vigilant and faithful, sentineled in the soul, guarding against violence to peace and life. But whilst so much is freely accorded to feeling in the economy of human welfare, something more than feeling is necessary to grapple with a fact so grim and significant as was this raid. Viewed apart and alone, as a transaction separate and distinct from its antecedents and bearings, it takes rank with the most cold-blooded and atrocious wrongs ever perpetrated; but just here is the trouble, this raid on Harpers Ferry, no more than Sherman's March to the Sea,[110] can consent to be thus viewed alone.

---

110 At the end of 1864, Major General William Tecumseh Sherman led Union troops from Atlanta to Savannah, Georgia, ferociously destroying military targets, infrastructure, and civilian property along the way.

There is, in the world's government, a force which has in all ages been recognized, sometimes as Nemesis,[111] sometimes as the judgment of God and sometimes as retributive justice; but under whatever name, all history attests the wisdom and beneficence of its chastisements, and men become reconciled to the agents through whom it operates, and have extolled them as heroes, benefactors and demigods.

To the broad vision of a true philosophy, nothing in this world stands alone. Everything is a necessary part of everything else. The margin of chance is narrowed by every extension of reason and knowledge, and nothing comes unbidden to the feast of human experience. The universe, of which we are a part, is continually proving itself a stupendous whole, a system of law and order, eternal and perfect. Every seed bears fruit after its kind, and nothing is reaped which was not sowed. The distance between seed time and harvest, in the moral world, may not be quite so well defined or as clearly intelligible as in the physical, but there is a seed time, and there is a harvest time, and though ages may intervene, and neither he who ploughed nor he who sowed may reap in person, yet the harvest nevertheless will surely come, and as in the physical world there are century plants, so it may be in the moral world, and their fruitage is as certain in the one as in the other. The bloody harvest

---

111 Greek goddess who punished overly proud mortals.

of Harpers Ferry was ripened by the heat and moisture of merciless bondage of more than two hundred years. That startling cry of alarm on the banks of the Potomac was but the answering back of the avenging angel to the midnight invasions of Christian slave-traders on the sleeping hamlets of Africa. The history of the African slave-trade furnishes many illustrations far more cruel and bloody.

Viewed thus broadly our subject is worthy of thoughtful and dispassionate consideration. It invites the study of the poet, scholar, philosopher and states-man. What the masters in natural science have done for man in the physical world, the masters of social science may yet do for him in the moral world. Science now tells us when storms are in the sky, and when and where their violence will be most felt. Why may we not yet know with equal certainty when storms are in the moral sky, and how to avoid their desolating force? But I can invite you to no such profound discussions. I am not the man, nor is this the occasion, for such philosophical enquiry. Mine is the word of grateful memory to an old friend; to tell you what I knew of him—what I knew of his inner life—of what he did and what he attempted, and thus if possible to make the mainspring of his ac-tions manifest and thereby give you a clearer view of his character and services.

It is said that next in value to the performance of great deeds ourselves is the capacity to appreciate such when performed by others; to more than this I do not presume. Allow me one other personal word before I proceed. In the minds of some of the American people I was myself credited with an important agency in the John Brown raid. Governor Henry A. Wise[112] was manifestly of that opinion. He was at the pains of having Mr. Buchanan send his Marshals to Rochester to invite me to accompany them to Virginia. *I did not happen to see them.*[113] *[Laughter.]*

What ground there was for this distinguished consideration shall duly appear in the natural course of this lecture. I wish however to say just here that there was no foundation whatever for the charge that I in any wise urged or instigated John Brown to his dangerous work. I rejoice that it is my good fortune to have seen, not only the end of slavery, but to see the day when the whole truth can be told about this matter without prejudice to either the living or the dead. I shall however allow myself little prominence in these disclosures. Your interests, like mine, are in the all-commanding figure of the story, and to him I consecrate the hour. His zeal in the

---

112 Governor of Virginia who was "determined to prove a national—indeed, a continental—conspiracy, one involving the black fugitives in Canada" (McFeely, *Frederick Douglass,* 200). In early 1861, Wise, a die-hard Confederate, was so eager to go to war that he planned his own raid on Harpers Ferry (which was preempted by the attack on Fort Sumter).

113 In the original version of the speech, Douglass said, "Fortunately I left town several hours previous to their arrival." According to McFeely (p. 200), the night before the marshals arrived, Douglass had hopped a boat to Canada, and a few weeks later (in mid-November 1859), he set sail from Nova Scotia to England.

cause of my race was far greater than mine—it was as the burning sun to my taper light—mine was bounded by time, his stretched away to the boundless shores of eternity. *I could talk for freedom; he could fight for it. I could live for the slave, but he could die for him. [Applause.]* The crown of martyrdom is high, far beyond the reach of ordinary mortals, and yet happily no special greatness or superior moral excellence is necessary to discern and in some measure appreciate a truly great soul. Cold, calculating and unspiritual as most of us are, we are not wholly insensible to real greatness; and when we are brought in contact with a man of commanding mold, towering high and alone above the millions, free from all conventional fetters, true to his own moral convictions, a "law unto himself," ready to suffer misconstruction, ignoring torture and death for what he believes to be right, we are compelled to do him homage.

In the stately shadow, in the sublime presence of such a soul I find myself standing tonight; and how to do it reverence, how to do it justice, how to honor the dead with due regard to the living, has been a matter of most anxious solicitude.

Much has been said of John Brown, much that is wise and beautiful, but in looking over what may be called the John Brown literature, I have been little assisted with material, and even less encouraged with any hope of success in treating the subject. Scholarship, genius and devotion have hastened with poetry and eloquence, story and song to this simple altar of human virtue, and have retired dissatisfied and distressed with the thinness and poverty of their offerings, as I shall with mine.

The difficulty in doing justice to the life and character of such a man is not altogether due to the quality of the zeal, or of the ability brought to the work, nor yet to any imperfections in the qualities of the man himself; the state of the moral atmosphere about us has much to do with it. The fault is not in our eyes, nor yet in the object, if under a murky sky we fail to discover the object. Wonderfully tenacious is the taint of a great wrong. The evil, as well as "the good that men do, lives after them."[114] Slavery is indeed gone; but its long, black shadow yet falls broad and large over the face of the whole country. It is the old truth oft-repeated, and never more fitly than now, "a prophet is without honor in his own country and among his own people."[115] Though more than twenty years have rolled between us and the Harpers Ferry raid, though since then the armies of the nation have found it necessary to do on a large scale what John Brown attempted to do on a small one, and the great captain who fought his way through slavery has filled with honor the presidential chair,[116] we yet stand too near the days of slavery, and the life and times

---

114 From *Julius Caesar*.
115 From Matthew 13:57.
116 Ulysses S. Grant.

of John Brown, to see clearly the true martyr and hero that he was and rightly to estimate the value of the man and his works.

Like the great and good of all ages—the men born in advance of their times, the men whose bleeding footprints attest the immense cost of reform, and show us the long and dreary spaces, between the luminous points in the progress of mankind—this our noblest American hero must wait the polishing wheels of after-coming centuries to make his glory more manifest, and his worth more generally acknowledged. Such instances are abundant and familiar. If we go back four and twenty centuries, to the stately city of Athens, and search among her architectural splendor and her miracles of art for the Socrates of today, and as he stands in history, we shall find ourselves perplexed and disappointed. In Jerusalem, Jesus himself was only the "carpenter's son"—a young man wonderfully destitute of worldly prudence, a pestilent fellow, "inexcusably and perpetually interfering in the world's business," "upsetting the tables of the money-changers," preaching sedition, opposing the good old religion, "making himself greater than Abraham," and at the same time "keeping company" with very low people. But behold the change! He was a great miracle-worker, in his day, but time has worked for him a greater miracle than all his miracles, for now his name stands for all that is desirable in government, noble in life, orderly and beautiful in society.

That which time has done for other great men of his class, that will time certainly do for John Brown. The brightest gems shine at first with subdued light, and the strongest characters are subject to the same limitations. Under the influence of adverse education and hereditary bias, few things are more difficult than to render impartial justice. Men hold up their hands to Heaven, and swear they will do justice, but what are oaths against prejudice and against inclination! In the face of high-sounding professions and affirmations we know well how hard it is for a Turk to do justice to a Christian, or for a Christian to do justice to a Jew. How hard for an Englishman to do justice to an Irishman, for an Irishman to do justice to an Englishman, harder still for an American tainted by slavery to do justice to the Negro or the Negro's friends. *[Applause.]* "John Brown," said the late William H. Seward, "was justly hanged." "John Brown," said the late Governor [John A.] Andrew of Massachusetts, "was right." *[Applause.] One [opinion] was from an aspirant to the presidency, a disease that warps the judgment of the best of men; the other that of the noblest heart and truest spirit of a noble state. [Applause.]*

Through all the turmoil and peril there was one who knew no fear—Wendell Phillips [applause], who never quailed or halted in the hour of danger, and one who remembered those in bonds as if bound with them. There, too, was the voice of a saluted woman, Lydia Maria

Childs, lifted up in clear, unfaltering tones for right and freedom. Phillips came to New York, and excluded from all meeting places there, he crossed over Brooklyn ferry, where he found one man brave like himself, who gave his pulpit as a speaking ground, Henry Ward Beecher. [Applause.] But sympathy arose in the land for John Brown above all the turmoil and rage. "Hang him," said Ralph Waldo Emerson, "and you will make him glorious like the cross."

There is, however, one aspect of the present subject quite worthy of notice, for it makes the hero of Harpers Ferry in some degree an exception to the general rules to which I have just now adverted. Despite the hold which slavery had at that time on the country, despite the popular prejudice against the Negro, despite the shock which the first alarm occasioned, almost from the first John Brown received a large measure of sympathy and appreciation. New England recognized in him the spirit which brought the pilgrims to Plymouth rock and hailed him as a martyr and saint. True, he had broken the law; true, he had struck for a despised people; true, he had crept upon his foe stealthily, like a wolf upon the fold, and had dealt his blow in the dark whilst his enemy slept. But with all this and more to disturb the moral sense, men discerned in him the greatest and best qualities known to human nature, and pronounced him "good." Many consented to his death, and then went home and taught their children to sing his praise as one whose "soul is marching on" through the realms of endless bliss.[117]

The country had before this learned the value of Brown's heroic character. He had shown boundless courage and skill in dealing with the enemies of liberty in Kansas.[118] With men so few, and means so small, and odds against him so great, no captain ever surpassed him in achievements, some of which seem almost beyond belief. With only eight men in that bitter war, he met, fought and captured [militia leader] Henry Clay Pate, [who had] 25 well-armed and mounted men. In this memorable encounter, he selected his ground so wisely, handled his men so skillfully, and attacked the enemy so vigorously, that they could neither run nor fight, and were therefore compelled to surrender to a force less than one-third their own. With just thirty men on another important occasion during the same border war, he met and vanquished four hundred Missourians under the command of Gen. [John W.] Reid. These men had come into the territory under an oath never to return to their homes till they had stamped out the last vestige of Free State spirit in Kansas; but a brush with old Brown took this high conceit out of them, and they were glad to get off upon any terms, without stopping

---

117 Reference to the lyrics of "John Brown's Body."

118 During 1856–1859, Brown waged a series of violent confrontations with proslavery forces in Kansas. Most notably, he presided over a brutal slaughter of a family of proslavery settlers, and ultimately lost two of his sons in the skirmishes.

to stipulate. With less than one hundred men to defend the town of Lawrence, he offered to lead them and give battle to fourteen hundred men on the banks of the Wakarusa River, and was much vexed when his offer was refused by Gen. Jim Lane and others to whom the defense of the town was confided. Before leaving Kansas, he went into the border of Missouri, and liberated a dozen slaves in a single night, and, in spite of slave laws and marshals, he brought these people through a half dozen States, and landed them safely in Canada, *and I happened to be with him when did it.*[119] *[Applause.]*

With eighteen men [at Harpers Ferry] this man shook the whole social fabric of Virginia. With eighteen men he overpowered a town of nearly three thousand souls. With these eighteen men he held that large community firmly in his grasp for thirty long hours. With these eighteen men he rallied in a single night fifty slaves to his standard, and made prisoners of an equal number of the slave-holding class. With these eighteen men he defied the power and bravery of a dozen of the best militia companies that Virginia could send against him. Now, when slavery struck, as it certainly did strike, at the life of the country, it was not the fault of John Brown that our rulers did not at first know how to deal

---

119 In *John Brown: The Cost of Freedom*, DeCaro explains that en route to Chatham, Ontario, with the liberated slaves in March 1859, Brown met with Douglass in Detroit, where the latter was giving a lecture (pp. 63–69). There is no record of Douglass going to Canada with Brown.

with it. He had already shown us the weak side of the rebellion, had shown us where to strike and how. It was not from lack of native courage that Virginia submitted for thirty long hours and at last was relieved only by Federal troops; but because the attack was made on the side of her conscience and thus armed her against herself. She beheld at her side the sullen brow of a black Ireland. When John Brown proclaimed emancipation to the slaves of Maryland and Virginia he added to his war power the force of a moral earthquake. Virginia felt all her strong-ribbed mountains to shake under the heavy tread of armed insurgents. Of his army of 19 her conscience made an army of 1,900.

Another feature of the times, worthy of notice, was the effect of this blow upon the country at large. At the first moment we were stunned and bewildered. Slavery had so benumbed the moral sense of the nation that it never suspected the possibility of an explosion like this, and it was difficult for Capt. Brown to get himself taken for what he really was. Few could seem to comprehend that freedom to the slaves was his only object. If you will go back with me to that time you will find that the most curious and contradictory versions of the affair were industriously circulated, and those which were the least rational and true seemed to command the readiest belief. In the view of some, it assumed tremendous proportions. To such it was nothing less than a wide-sweeping rebellion to overthrow the existing government, and construct another upon its ruins, with Brown for its president and commander-in-chief, the proof of this was found in the old man's carpetbag in the shape of a constitution for a new republic, an instrument which in reality had been executed to govern the conduct of his men in the mountains.[120] Smaller and meaner natures saw in it nothing higher than a purpose to plunder. To them John Brown and his men were a gang of desperate robbers, who had learned by some means that [the] government had sent a large sum of money to Harpers Ferry to pay off the workmen in its employ there, and they had gone thence to fill their pockets from this money.

The fact is that outside of a few friends, scattered in different parts of the country, and the slave-holders of Virginia, few persons understood the significance of the hour. That a man might do something very audacious and desperate for money, power or fame was to the general apprehension quite possible; but, in face of plainly-written law, in face of constitutional guarantees protecting each state against domestic violence, in face of a nation of 40 million people, that 19 men could invade a great state to liberate a despised and hated race,

---

120 At a May 1858 convention in Chatham, Ontario, Brown—along with Martin Delany and several other black participants—debated, then agreed to, a "Provisional Constitution" for an interracial government, forming the basis of a state that would be a haven for runaway slaves in the Alleghenies. Brown had drawn up his original blueprint while staying at Douglass's home in Rochester earlier that year, but Douglass did not attend the convention. See DeCaro, 59–62.

was to the average intellect and conscience, too monstrous for belief. In this respect the vision of Virginia was
clearer than that of the nation. Conscious of her guilt and
therefore full of suspicion, sleeping on pistols for pillows,
startled at every unusual sound, constantly fearing and
expecting a repetition of the Nat Turner insurrection [of
1831], she at once understood the meaning, if not the
magnitude of the affair. It was this understanding which
caused her to raise the lusty and imploring cry to the
federal government for help, and it was not till he who
struck the blow had fully explained his motives and object that the incredulous nation in any [way] compre-
hended the true spirit of the raid, or of its commander.

Fortunate for his memory, fortunate for the brave
men associated with him, fortunate for the truth of history, John Brown survived the saber gashes, bayonet
wounds and bullet holes, and was able, though covered
with blood, to tell his own story and make his own defense. Had he with all his men, as might have been the
case, gone down in the shock of battle, the world would
have had no true basis for its judgment, and one of the
most heroic efforts ever witnessed in behalf of liberty
would have been confounded with base and selfish pur-
poses. When, like savages, [Gov. Wise and company]
stood around the fallen and bleeding hero, and sought
by torturing questions to wring from his supposed dying lips some word by which to soil the sublime un-

dertaking, by implicating [the Secret Six[121]] and other prominent anti-slavery men, the brave old man not only avowed his object to be the emancipation of the slaves, but serenely and proudly announced himself as solely responsible for all that had happened. Though some thought of his own life might at such a moment have seemed natural and excusable, he showed none, and scornfully rejected the idea that he acted as the agent or instrument of any man or set of men. He admitted that he had friends and sympathizers, but to his own head he invited all the bolts of slavehold[er] wrath and fury, and welcomed them to do their worst. His manly courage and self-forgetful nobleness were not lost upon the crowd about him, nor upon the country. They drew applause from his bitterest enemies. Said Henry A. Wise, "He is the gamest man I ever met." "He was kind and humane to his prisoners," said Col. Lewis Washington.[122]

To the outward eye of men, John Brown was a criminal, but to their inward eye he was a just man and true. His deeds might be disowned, but the spirit which made those deeds possible was worthy [of the] highest honor. It has been often asked, why did not Virginia spare the life of this man? Why did she not avail herself of this

---

121 The Secret Six, or primary fundraisers for Brown's raid on Harpers Ferry, were Gerrit Smith, Thomas Wentworth Higginson, Theodore Parker, and three men from the Boston area, Dr. Samuel G. Howe (married to Julia Ward Howe, who penned "John Brown's Body"), Franklin Sanborn, and George L. Stearns.
122 Colonel Lewis Washington, a great-grandnephew of the first president, was taken hostage during the Harpers Ferry raid.

grand opportunity to add to her other glory that of a lofty magnanimity? [They could have] spared the good old man's life, and said to him: "You see we have you in our power, and could easily take your life, but we have no desire to hurt you in any way; you have committed a terrible crime against society; you have invaded us at midnight and attacked a sleeping community, but we recognize you as a fanatic, and in some sense instigated by others; and on this ground and others, we release you. Go about your business, and tell those who sent you that we can afford to be magnanimous to our enemies." I say, had Virginia held some such language as this to John Brown, she would have inflicted a heavy blow on the whole Northern abolition movement, one which only the omnipotence of truth and the force of truth could have overcome. I have no doubt Gov. Wise would have done so gladly, but, alas, he was the executive of a state which thought she could not afford such magnanimity. She had that within her bosom which could more safely tolerate the presence of a criminal than a saint, a highway robber than a moral hero. All her hills and valleys were studded with material for a disastrous conflagration, and one spark of the dauntless spirit of Brown might set the whole state in flames. A sense of this appalling liability put an end to every noble consideration. His death was a foregone conclusion, and his trial was simply one of form.

Honor to the brave young Col. [George Henry]

Hoyt who hastened from Massachusetts to defend his friend's life at the peril of his own; but there would have been no hope of success had he been allowed to plead the case. He might have surpassed [Rufus] Choate or [Daniel] Webster in power—a thousand physicians might have sworn that Capt. Brown was insane, [but] it would have been all to no purpose, [as] neither eloquence nor testimony could have prevailed. Slavery was the idol of Virginia, and pardon and life to Brown meant condemnation and death to slavery. He had practically illustrated a truth stranger than fiction—a truth higher than Virginia had ever known, a truth more noble and beautiful than Jefferson ever wrote. He had evinced a conception of the sacredness and value of liberty which transcended in sublimity that of her own Patrick Henry and made even his fire-flashing sentiment of "Liberty or Death" seem dark and tame and selfish. Henry loved liberty for himself, but this man loved liberty for all men, and for those most despised and scorned, as well as for those most esteemed and honored. Just here was the true glory of John Brown's mission. It was not for his own freedom that he was thus ready to lay down his life, for with Paul he could say, "I was born free." No chain had bound his ankle, no yoke had galled his neck. History has no better illustration of pure, disinterested benevolence. It was not Caucasian for Caucasian, a white man for white man; not rich man for rich man; but Caucasian for Ethiopian—a white man for black man, a rich man for poor man; the man admitted and respected, for the man despised and rejected.

"I want you to understand, gentlemen," [Brown] said to his persecutors, "that I respect the rights of the poorest and weakest of the colored people, oppressed by the slave system, as I do those of the most wealthy and powerful."[123] In this we have the key to the whole life and career of the man. Than in this sentiment humanity has nothing more touching, reason nothing more noble, imagination nothing more sublime—and if we could reduce all the religions of the world to one essence, we could find in it nothing more divine. It is much to be regretted that some great artist, in sympathy with the spirit of the occasion, had not been present when these and similar words were spoken. The situation was thrilling. An old man in the center of an excited and angry crowd, far away from home, in an enemy's country—with no friend near—overpowered, defeated, wounded, bleeding, covered with reproaches his brave companions nearly all dead, his two faithful sons stark and cold by his side; reading his death-warrant in his fast-oozing blood and increasing weakness as in the faces of all around him; yet calm, collected, brave, with a heart for any fate, using his supposed dying moments to

---

123 Brown said this shortly after his capture, as he lay wounded in a hospital bed. He was being interrogated by a group including Ohio Representative Clement Vallandigham, a leading proslavery Democrat who whipped up anti-Brown hostilities.

explain his course and vindicate his cause: such a subject would have been at once an inspiration and a power for one of the grandest historical pictures ever painted.

With John Brown, as with every other man fit to die for a cause, the hour of his physical weakness was the hour of his moral strength, the hour of his defeat was the hour of his triumph, the moment of his capture was the crowning victory of his life. With the Allegheny mountains for his pulpit, the country for his church and the whole civilized world for his audience, he was a thousand times more effective as a preacher than as a warrior, and the consciousness of this fact was the secret of his amazing complacency. Mighty with the sword of steel, he was mightier with the sword of the truth, and with this sword he literally swept the horizon. He was more than a match for [any] who could rise against him. They could kill him, but they could not answer him.

In studying the character and works of a great man, it is always desirable to learn in what he is distinguished from others, and what have been the causes of this difference. Such men as he whom we are now considering come on to the theater of life only at long intervals. It is not always easy to explain the exact and logical causes that produce them, the subtle influences which sustain them, [or] the immense heights where we sometimes find them; but we know that the hour and the man are seldom far apart, and that here, as elsewhere, the demand may in some mysterious way regulate the supply. A great iniquity, hoary with age, proud and defiant, tainting the whole moral atmosphere of the country, subjecting both church and state to its control, demanded the startling shock which John Brown seemed especially inspired to give it.

Apart from this mission there was nothing very remarkable about him. He was a wool-dealer, and a good judge of wool, as a wool-dealer ought to be. In all visible respects he was a man like unto other men. No outward sign of Kansas or Harpers Ferry was about him. As I knew him, he was an even-tempered man, neither morose, malicious nor misanthropic, but kind, amiable, courteous, and gentle in his intercourse with men. His words were few, well chosen and forcible. He was a good business man, and a good neighbor. A good friend, a good citizen, a good husband and father: a man apparently in every way calculated to make a smooth and pleasant path for himself through the world. He loved society, he loved little children, he liked music, and was fond of animals. To no one was the world more beautiful or life more sweet. How then as I have said shall we explain his apparent indifference to life? I can find but one answer, and that is, his intense hatred to oppression. I have talked with many men, but I remember none who seemed so deeply excited upon the subject of slavery as he. He would walk the room in agitation at mention of the word. He saw the evil through no mist or haze, but in a light of infinite brightness, which left no line of its ten thousand horrors out of sight. Law, religion, learning, were interposed in its behalf in vain.

Against truth and right, legislative enactments were to his mind mere cobwebs—the pompous emptiness of human pride, the pitiful out-breathings of human nothingness. He used to say, "Whenever there is a right thing to be done, there is a 'thus saith the Lord' that it shall be done."

It must be admitted that Brown assumed tremendous responsibility in making war upon the peaceful people of Harpers Ferry, but it must be remembered also that in his eye a slave-holding community could not be peaceable, but was, in the nature of the case, in one incessant state of war. To him such a community was not more sacred than a band of robbers: it was the right of anyone to assault it by day or night. He saw no hope that slavery would ever be abolished by moral or political means. He knew, he said, "the proud and hard hearts of the slave-holders, and that they never would consent to give up their slaves, till they felt a big stick about their heads." It was five years before this event at Harpers Ferry, while the conflict between freedom and slavery was waxing hotter and hotter with every hour, that the blundering statesmanship of the national government repealed the Missouri Compromise,[124] and thus launched the territory of Kansas as a prize to be

---

124 The Kansas–Nebraska Act of 1854 repealed the Missouri Compromise of 1820, thus allowing slavery to expand into the West.

battled for between the North and the South. The remark-able part taken in this contest by Brown has been already referred to, and it doubtless helped to prepare him for the final tragedy, and though it did not by any means originate the plan, it confirmed him in it and hastened its execution.

During his four years' service in Kansas it was my good fortune to see him often. On his trips to and from the territory he sometimes stopped several days at my house, and at one time several weeks. It was on this last occasion that liberty had been victorious in Kansas, and he felt that he must hereafter devote himself to what he considered his larger work. It was the theme of all his conversation, filling his nights with dreams and his days with visions. An incident of his boyhood may explain, in some measure, the intense abhorrence he felt to slav-ery. He had for some reason been sent into the state of Kentucky, where he made the acquaintance of a slave boy, about his own age, of whom he became very fond. For some petty offense this boy was one day subjected to a brutal beating. The blows were dealt with an iron shovel and fell fast and furiously upon his slender body. Born in a free state and unaccustomed to such scenes of cruelty, young Brown's pure and sensitive soul revolted at the shocking spectacle and at that early age he swore eternal hatred to slavery. After years never obliterated the impression, and he found in this early experience an argument against contempt for small things. It is true that the boy is the father of the man.

Most of us can remember some event or incident which has at some time come to us, and made itself a permanent part of our lives. Such an incident came to me in the year 1847.[125] I had then the honor of spending a day and a night under the roof of a man whose character and conversation made a very deep impression on my mind and heart; and as the circumstance does not lie entirely out of the range of our present observations, you will pardon for a moment a seeming digression. The name of the person alluded to had been several times mentioned to me, in a tone that made me curious to see him and to make his acquaintance. He was a [wool] merchant, and our first meeting was at his store—a substantial brick building, giving evidence of a flourishing business. After a few minutes' detention here, long enough for me to observe the neatness and order of the place, I was conducted by him to his residence where I was kindly received by his family as an expected guest.

I was a little disappointed at the appearance of this man's house, for after seeing his fine store, I was prepared to see a fine residence; but this logic was entirely contradicted by the facts. The house was a small, wooden one, on a back street in a neighborhood of laboring men and mechanics—respectable enough, but not just the spot where one would expect to find the home of a success-

---

125 According to David S. Reynolds, Douglass "interrupted a lecture tour in November 1847 to visit the Brown home" (in Springfield, Massachusetts). Reynolds, *John Brown, Abolitionist*, (New York: Knopf, 2005), 103.

ful merchant. Plain as was the outside, the inside was plainer. Its furniture might have pleased a Spartan. It would take longer to tell what was not in it, than what was—no sofas, no cushions, no curtains, no carpets, no easy rocking chairs inviting to enervation or rest or repose. My first meal passed under the misnomer of tea. It was none of your tea and toast sort, but potatoes and cabbage, and beef soup, such a meal as a man might relish after following the plough all day, or after performing a forced march of a dozen miles over rough ground in frosty weather. Innocent of paint, veneering, varnish or tablecloth, the table announced itself unmistakably and honestly pine and of the plainest workmanship. No hired help passed from kitchen to dining room, staring in amazement at the colored man at the white man's table. The mother, daughters and sons did the serving, and did it well. I heard no apology for doing their own work; they went through it as if used to it, untouched by any thought of degradation or impropriety.

Supper over, the boys helped to clear the table and wash the dishes. This style of housekeeping struck me as a little odd. I mention it because household management is worthy of thought. A house is more than brick and mortar, wood or paint; this to me at least was. In its plainness it was a truthful reflection of its inmates: no disguises, no illusions, no make-believes here, but stern truth and solid purpose breathed in all its arrangements. I was not long in company with the master of this house before I discovered that he was indeed the master of it, and likely to become mine too, if I stayed long with him. He fulfilled St. Paul's idea of the head of the family—his wife believed in him, and his children observed him with reverence. Whenever he spoke, his words commanded earnest attention. His arguments which I ventured at some points to oppose, seemed to convince all, his appeals touched all, and his will impressed all. Certainly I never felt myself in the presence of a stronger religious influence than while in this house. "God and duty, God and duty" [ran] like a thread of gold through all his utterances, and his family supplied a ready "Amen."

In person he was lean and sinewy, of the best New England mold, built for times of trouble, fitted to grapple with the flintiest hardships. Clad in plain American wool, shod in boots of cowhide leather, and wearing a cravat of the same substantial material, under six feet high, less than one hundred and fifty lbs. in weight, aged about fifty, he presented a figure straight and symmetrical as a mountain pine. His bearing was singularly impressive. His head was not large, but compact and high. His hair was coarse, strong, slightly gray and closely trimmed and grew close to his forehead. His face was smoothly shaved and revealed a strong square mouth, supported by a broad and prominent chin. His eyes were clear and grey, and in conversation they alternated with tears and fire. When on the street, he moved with a long springing, race-horse step, absorbed by his own reflections, neither seeking nor shunning observation.

Such was the man whose name I heard uttered in whispers, such was the house in which he lived, such were his family and household management—and such was Captain John Brown. He said to me at this meeting that he had invited me to his house for the special purpose of laying before me his plan for the speedy emancipation of my race. He seemed to apprehend opposition on my part as he opened the subject and touched my vanity by saying that he had observed my course at home and abroad, and wanted my co-operation. He said he had been for the last thirty years looking for colored men to whom he could safely reveal his secret, and had almost despaired, at times, of finding such, but that now he was encouraged for he saw heads rising up in all directions, to whom he thought he could with safety impart his plan. As this plan then lay in his mind it was very simple, and had much to commend it. It did not, as was supposed by many, contemplate a general rising among the slaves, and a general slaughter of the slave masters (an insurrection he thought would only defeat the object), but it did contemplate the creating of an armed force which should act in the very heart of the South. He was not averse to the shedding of blood, and thought the practice of carrying arms would be a good one for the colored people to adopt, as it would give them a sense of manhood. No people, he said, could have self-respect or be respected who would not fight for their freedom.

He called my attention to a large map of the US, and pointed out to me the far-reaching Alleghenies, stretching away from the borders of New York into the Southern states. "These mountains," he said, "are the basis of my plan. God has given the strength of these hills to freedom; they were placed here to aid the emancipation of your race; they are full of natural forts, where one man for defense would be equal to a hundred for attack; they are also full of good hiding places where a large number of men could be concealed and baffle and elude pursuit for a long time. I know these mountains well and could take a body of men into them and keep them there in spite of all the efforts of Virginia to dislodge me, and drive me out. I would take at first about twenty-five picked men and begin on a small scale, supply them arms and ammunition, post them in squads of fives on a line of twenty-five miles, these squads to busy themselves for a time in gathering recruits from the surrounding farms, seeking and selecting the most restless and daring."

He saw that in this part of the work the utmost care must be used to guard against treachery and disclosure; only the most conscientious and skillful should be sent on this perilous duty. With care and enterprise he thought he could soon gather a force of one hundred hardy men, men who would be content to lead the free and adventurous life to which he proposed to train them. When once properly drilled and each had found the place for which he was best suited, they would begin work in earnest; they would run off the slaves in large numbers, retain the strong and brave ones in the mountains, and send the weak and timid ones to the North by the Underground Railroad. His operations would be enlarged with increasing numbers and would not be confined to one locality. Slaveholders should in some cases be approached at midnight and told to give up their slaves and to let them have their best horses to ride away upon. Slavery was a state of war, he said, to which the slaves were unwilling parties and consequently they had a right to anything necessary to their peace and freedom.

He would shed no blood and would avoid a fight except in self-defense, when he would of course do his best. He believed this movement would weaken slavery in two ways: first, by making slave property insecure, it would become undesirable; and secondly, it would keep the anti-slavery agitation alive and public attention fixed upon it, and thus lead to the adoption of measures to abolish the evil altogether. He held that there was need of something startling to prevent the agitation of the question from dying out; that slavery had come near being abolished in Virginia by the Nat Turner insurrection, and he thought his method would speedily put an end to it, both in Maryland and Virginia. The trouble was to get the right men to start with and money enough to equip them. He had adopted the simple and economical mode of living to which I have referred with a view to save money for this purpose. This was said in no boastful tone, for he felt that he had delayed already too long and had no room to boast either his zeal or his self-denial.

From eight o'clock in the evening till three in the morning, Capt. Brown and I sat face to face, he arguing in favor of his plan, and I finding all the objections I could against it. Now mark! This meeting of ours was a full twelve years before the strike at Harpers Ferry. He had been watching and waiting all that time for suit-able heads to rise or "pop up" as he said among the sable millions in whom he could confide; hence forty years had passed between his thought and his act. Forty years, though not a long time in the life of a nation, is a long time in the life of a man; and here forty long years, this man was struggling with this one idea; like Moses he was forty years in the wilderness. Youth, manhood, middle age had come and gone; two marriages had been consummated, twenty children had called him father; and through all the storms and vicissitudes of busy life, this one thought, like the angel in the burning bush, had confronted him with its blazing light, bidding him on to his work. Like Moses he had made excuses, and as with Moses his excuses were overruled. Nothing should postpone further what was to him a divine command, the performance of which seemed to him his only apology for existence. He often said to me, though life was sweet to him, he would willingly lay it down for the freedom of my people; and on one occasion he added, that he had already lived about as long as most men, since he had slept less, and if he should now lay down his life the loss would not be great, for in fact, he knew no better.

Two weeks prior to the meditated attack, Capt. Brown summoned me to meet him in an old stone quarry on the Conococheague [Creek], near the town of Chambersburg, Pennsylvania. His arms and ammunition were stored in that town and were to be moved on to Harpers Ferry. In company with Shields Green I obeyed the summons, and prompt to the hour we met the dear old man, with [John] Kagi, his secretary, at the appointed place.[126] Our meeting was in some sense a council of war. We spent the Saturday and succeeding Sunday in conference on the question [of] whether the desperate step should then be taken, or the old plan as already described should be carried out. [Brown] was for boldly striking Harpers Ferry at once and running the risk of getting into the mountains afterwards. I was for avoiding Harpers Ferry altogether. Shields Green and Mr.

---

126 Shields Green is described in the subsequent paragraph. Kagi, a white abolitionist from Ohio, had fought together with Brown since the initial Kansas battles in 1856 and was his second-in-command. He agreed with the raid on Harpers Ferry, but advocated a quick strike, then a retreat to the mountains. He was killed while trying to flee after the raid. See Reynolds, *John Brown*, Chap. 12.

Kagi remained silent listeners throughout. It is needless to repeat here what was said, after what has happened. Suffice it, that after all I could say, I saw that my old friend had resolved on his course and that it was idle to parley. I told him finally that it was impossible for me to join him. I could see Harpers Ferry only as a trap of steel, and ourselves on the wrong side of it. He regretted my decision and we parted.

Thus far, I have spoken exclusively of Capt. Brown. Let me say a word or two of his brave and devoted men, and first of Shields Green. He was a fugitive slave from Charleston, South Carolina, and had attested his love of liberty by escaping from slavery and making his way through many dangers to Rochester, where he had lived in my family, and where he met the man with whom he went to the scaffold. I said to him, as I was about to leave, "Now Shields, you have heard our discussion. If in view of it, you do not wish to stay, you have but to say so, and you can go back with me." He answered, "I b'l'eve I'll go wid de ole man"; and go with him he did, into the fight, and to the gallows, and bore himself as grandly as any of the number. At the moment when Capt. Brown was surrounded, and all chance of escape was cut off, Green was in the mountains and could have made his escape as Osborne Anderson[127] did, but

---

127 Born in Chester County, Pennsylvania, Anderson was the only black survivor of the Harpers Ferry raid, escaping (with Albert Hazlett, a white accomplice also from Pennsylvania) via a stolen boat through Maryland to Pennsylvania.

when asked to do so, he made the same answer he did at Chambersburg, "I b'l'eve I'll go down wid de ole man." When in prison at Charlestown, and he was not allowed to see his old friend, his fidelity to him was in no [way] weakened, and no complaint against Brown could be extorted from him by those who talked with him.

If a monument should be erected to the memory of John Brown, as there ought to be, the form and name of Shields Green should have a conspicuous place upon it. It is a remarkable fact that in this small company of men, but one showed any sign of weakness or regret for what he did or attempted to do. Poor Cook broke down and sought to save his life by representing that he had been deceived, and allured by false promises. But Stephens, Hazlett and Green went to their doom like the heroes they were, without a murmur, without a regret, believing alike in their captain and their cause.[128]

For the disastrous termination of this invasion, several causes have been assigned. It has been said that Capt. Brown found it necessary to strike before he was ready; that men had promised to join him from the North who failed to arrive; that the cowardly Negroes did not rally to his support as he expected. But the true

---

128 John Cook was from Connecticut but had served as a law clerk in Brooklyn before joining Brown in Kansas; once caught in Harpers Ferry, he wrote a public confession that implicated Douglass (although this did not stop Cook from being executed). A seasoned soldier, Aaron Stevens was also from Connecticut, and shared a cell with Brown. Unlike Anderson, Hazlett did not successfully escape, and after his capture in Carlisle, Pennsylvania, he was executed with Stevens.

cause as stated by himself, contradicts all these theories, and from his statement there is no appeal. Among the questions put to him by Mr. Vallandigham after his capture were the following: "Did you expect a general uprising of the slaves in case of your success?" To this he answered, "No, sir, nor did I wish it. I expected to gather strength from time to time and then to set them free." "Did you expect to hold possession here until then?" Answer, "Well, probably I had quite a different idea. I do not know as I ought to reveal my plans. I am here wounded and a prisoner because I foolishly permitted myself to be so. You overstate your strength when you suppose I could have been taken if I had not allowed it. I was too tardy after commencing the open attack in delaying my movements through Monday night and up to the time of the arrival of government troops. It was all because of my desire to spare the feelings of my prisoners and their families."

But the question is: Did John Brown fail? He certainly did fail to get out of Harpers Ferry before being beaten down by United States soldiers; he did fail to save his own life, and to lead a liberating army into the mountains of Virginia. But he did not go to Harpers Ferry to save his life. The true question is: Did John Brown draw his sword against slavery and thereby lose his life in vain? And to this I answer ten thousand times, No! No man fails, or can fail, who so grandly gives himself and all he has to a righteous cause. No man, who in his hour of [most] extreme need, when on his way to meet an ignominious death, could so forget himself as to stop and kiss a little child, one of the hated race for whom he was about to die, could by any possibility fail.[129] Did John Brown fail? Ask Henry A. Wise, in whose house less than two years after, a school for the emancipated slaves was taught. Did John Brown fail? Ask Clement L. Vallandigham, one other of the inquisitorial party, for he too went down in the tremendous whirlpool created by the powerful hand of this bold invader.

If John Brown did not end the war that ended slavery, he did at least begin the war that ended slavery. [*Applause.*] If we look over the dates, places and men, for which this honor is claimed, we shall find that not [South] Carolina, but Virginia; not Fort Sumter, but Harpers Ferry and the arsenal; [and] not Col. Anderson[130] but John Brown began the war that ended American slavery and made this a free republic. Until this blow was struck, the prospect for freedom was dim, shadowy and uncertain. The irrepressible conflict was one of words, votes and compromises. When John Brown stretched forth his arm the sky was cleared. The time for compromises was gone. [T]he armed hosts of

---

129 Brown biographer David S. Reynolds calls the story apocryphal. But given that Currier and Ives had made it the subject of a popular lithograph in 1884, few in the audience would have doubted its truth at the time. See Reynolds, *John Brown*, 392–393.

130 Major Robert Anderson was the Union officer in command of Fort Sumter during the 1861 attack.

freedom stood face to face over the chasm of a broken union, and failing to do that, drew the sword of rebellion and thus made her own, and not Brown's, the lost cause of the century.

A quartet of ladies and gentlemen sang all 17 stanzas of "John Brown's Body" after the address. Mr. Douglass helped them out and so did the audience.[131]

---

131 It was the *Brooklyn Times* account that noted that all seventeen stanzas were sung.

CHAPTER 8

LINCOLN'S GODLIKE NATURE

Crown Heights
February 1893

There was much enthusiasm when the venerable and picturesque figure of the famous colored orator slowly arose. He stood for several minutes looking upon the cheering group, with a smile of evident satisfaction upon his interesting features.
—New York Tribune, *February 14, 1893*

Douglass's final public appearance in Brooklyn came in February 1893, when the seventy-five-year-old statesman addressed an Abraham Lincoln Day celebration. Three hundred of Brooklyn's leading Republicans assembled at the clubhouse of the Union League, on Bedford Avenue in Crown Heights. The *Brooklyn Times* called the group "the chief social organization in Brooklyn," listing the names and table numbers of all the attendees. Before Douglass spoke, a ten-course dinner was served, commencing with Blue Point oysters.

After dessert, the cigars came out, and the *Eagle* described what happened next:

As the colored orator rose, the company rose with him, cheering, waving handkerchiefs and striking into the chorus of "For He's a Jolly Good Fellow" with a vim that made the candle-shades shake. Mr. Douglass had prepared a written speech, but before he began to read it, he expressed his pleasure in the warm welcome. He added: "I am under some embarrassment because the most difficult of all companies is an after-dinner company and I have little experience with after-dinner speeches. It is generally said that they must be short. But it so happens that I've never made a short speech which satisfied myself and have very seldom made a long one which satisfied anybody else."

Referring to the changed position of the Negro race, which made his presence at such a dinner possible, Douglass told of his experience with an old abolitionist who, years ago, met him on Broadway and taking his arm exclaimed: "Come, Douglass, let's go down the street. I am not ashamed to walk with you." Then the speaker added dryly: "It never seemed to occur to him for any reason that I might be ashamed to walk with him."[132]

---

132 *Brooklyn Times*, February 14, 1893.

Douglass had told the same anecdote at BAM in January 1866—and he had served up some of the Lincoln tales in his after-dinner talk on several occasions before. The retrospective quality of the speech, as well as the hearty response, made it seem like a farewell address.[133] And at least for Brooklyn audiences, it was, as Douglass would die of a heart attack just over two years later, in March of 1895.

Douglass once again urged his audience to honor the spirit of Lincoln by paying attention to the rising tide of discrimination and violence against blacks in the South. Here's an account of the speech from the *Brooklyn Standard Union*, a pro-Republican paper, which contains audience reactions. Additional notes from the *Eagle's* report are in italics.[134]

❊

Gentlemen—I beg to remind you at the outset that reminiscences are generally tedious. I hope you may find mine an exception to the general rule, though I fear the contrary, for speakers are often more interesting and eloquent about what they do not know than about what

---

133 According to McFeely, Douglass would deliver his "last great speech" at DC's Metropolitan AME Church in January 1894. The subject was lynching. *Frederick Douglass*, 371.

134 *Brooklyn Standard Union* and *Brooklyn Eagle*, February 14, 1893.

they do know. [*Applause.*] It is impossible for me and, perhaps, for anybody else, to say anything new about Abraham Lincoln. [*Applause.*] He is in the minds and hearts of all of us. We know him and know of him, as we know of no other great man of our century. [*Applause.*]

I had the good fortune to know Abraham Lincoln personally and peculiarly. I knew him, not on the side visible to the free, rich and powerful, but on the side which he presented to the unfortunate, defenseless, the oppressed and the enslaved. [*Applause.*]

It is something to know how a man will deport himself to his admitted equals, but more to know how he will bear himself to those who are recognized as his inferior. [*Applause.*] It is this knowledge of Mr. Lincoln upon which I depend for any interest, value or significance of my story to you this evening.

Of course, and on general principles, it is a great thing for any man of whatever condition to know a great man. For a truly great man is a rebuke to pride and selfishness in the strong, and a source of strength to the weak and unfortunate. The memory of such a great man is ennobling to men already noble, and we shall all feel better for reviving and keeping alive the memory of such a man tonight. [*Applause.*]

Gentlemen, let me be somewhat confidential and autobiographical. I have sometimes been held up as a man without friends or associates, but really I have been a very fortunate man during most of my life. Few men have had a chance to get more that is desirable and valuable out of this life than I. I have seen both sides of this great world. I have seen men of all conditions, I have seen men high and low, rich and poor, slave and free, white and black, and hence I ought to be a broader if not a better man, than most other men. I certainly have no excuse for narrowness or for race prejudice. I feel it more to be a man and a member of the great human family than to be a member of any one of the many varieties of the human race, whether Anglo-Saxon, Anglo-African, or any other.

Among the circumstances in which I deem myself most fortunate, is that of having seen many great men. They have not been of one country or of one continent alone. I have seen such men in England, and I have seen them in this republic. I have seen men of whom we have all heard; men who stood only a little lower than the angels.

Lincoln's Godlike Nature.
They were great and godlike men, divinely equipped and commissioned from on high to serve the highest needs of mankind. They were not only uplifted men, but they were uplifting men—men whose range was far above all that is little, low and mean—but I have met with no such man, at home or abroad, who made upon my mind the impression of possessing a more godlike nature than did Abraham Lincoln. [*Cheers and applause.*]

Greater men than he intellectually there may have been, but, to my mind measuring him in the direction of the highest quality, of human goodness and nobility of character, no better man than he has ever stood or walked upon the continent. [*Cheers.*] But you did not ask me for my opinion of Mr. Lincoln. [*Voice: "We're glad to get it."*] You asked me for my recollections of him, and, these I shall proceed to give you.

It may be that the conditions surrounding Mr. Lincoln when I first met him had something to do with the exalted impression I reserved of him. It is one thing to see a man in prosperity and another thing to see him in adversity. It is one thing to see him surrounded by hardships, difficulties and dangers, and it is another thing to see him in his hours of ease and prosperity.

The time to see a great captain is not when the wind is fair and the sea is smooth and the man in the crosstrees or round-top can safely sing out, "All is well." At such a time a pigmy may seem a giant and a poltroon a hero. You must see him under other conditions. You must see him when the sky is dark; see him in rough weather; see him in the hour of danger when he is far from land in mid-ocean, when his ship is in distress, tossed by the storm, engine disabled, rudder gone, sails blown away, stanchions staved in, mountain billows dashing over his deck. It is then, if ever, that you may know the true mettle of the man. If then you find him calm, collected, fearless and faithful, manly and undismayed, with no thought in his soul but the one thought of absolute and over-mastering duty, and determined to do that duty at whatever cost to himself or others, I say that you may then know that you are in the presence of a hero worthy of your highest human worship [*applause*], and such a captain was ours.

The sea was not smooth, the sky was not bright, the wind was not fair, when I first met and measured Abraham Lincoln. It was in the darkest hours of the late war. There was much in the situation to make men anxious. It was a time to make the boldest hold his breath. No man could tell, at that time, whether the cause of the country would be saved or lost, I certainly was concerned, not only for the cause of the country, but for the cause of the slave—a cause for which I had given the best energies of my soul, the best years of my life, and the deepest longings of my heart. [*Applause.*]

The leaders of the rebellion were at this time especially fierce, bold and defiant. They had, in the pride of their power, scorned to accept the terms of peace that Mr. Lincoln had a few months before offered them, whereby they might have saved the lives of many men on both sides, North and South, and their slavery in the bargain.

But it was not only the rebels in arms at the South, but also the disloyal men at the North, who complicated the problem, and gave Mr. Lincoln much cause for anxiety. Our forces in the field were diminishing. Recruiting was becoming difficult and well-nigh impossible. The draft was being resisted. Loyal black men were being murdered in the streets of New York. Asylums and houses of black people were being burned in resentment of the draft and of the continuance of the war. Besides, the administration was being fiercely assailed by the press, the platform and the pulpit of the North. Out of this darkness and storm the soul of Lincoln shone with a light all the more clear, calm and steady. [*Applause.*]

I first saw Mr. Lincoln in the early summer of 1863.[135] I had a special object in seeing him at this time. I had been engaged in raising two regiments of colored men in Massachusetts, the Fifty-fourth and Fifty-fifth. Two of my sons were in those regiments. Jefferson Davis had taken notice of those colored soldiers, and had notified the country that colored men taken in arms would not be treated as prisoners of war by the Confederate armies, but would be shot or hanged in cold blood, or sold into slavery. It was about this barbarous threat, in part, that I went to Washington to see Abraham Lincoln.

It required some nerve to approach the chief magistrate of the Nation for such a time. I did not know how he would receive a man of my complexion, or whether he would receive me at all. I was not a member of Congress, a United States marshal, a minister and

---

135 At the White House on August 10, 1863.

consul-general to Haiti, an elector at large, or even a citizen of the United States, [which] was still under the ban of the Dred Scott decision.[136] So I felt it a bold thing for me to enter the White House and presume to talk with the President of the United States. Besides, I had no one to introduce me. Happily I was soon relieved at this point. I met with the late [Kansas] Senator Samuel Pomeroy [*three cheers for Pomeroy*],[137] a good and true man, with whom I had become acquainted during the border-ruffian war in Kansas, and he kindly consented to accompany me to Mr. Lincoln. It was a daring thing for him, senator though he was, to walk the streets of Washington with me at that time. To do so was to invite insult.

This done, I went to the executive mansion, not however, without much solicitude as to how I should deport myself; how I should order my speech, and how this great man in his exalted office would be likely to receive and treat a man of my condition. The result was altogether at variance with my fears. I had not been an instant in the presence of this great man before all apprehensions were dispelled.

I saw before me a man, a great man, a tall man physically, and I was not long in discovering that I was

---

136 Owing to his Republican ties, Douglass worked with Congress while serving as president of the short-lived Freedmen's Savings Bank (1874). He was later US marshal for the District of Columbia (1877–1881) and minister to Haiti (1889–91); and he had been elector at large for New York State in the presidential election of 1872.

137 Pomeroy sat on the stage at Douglass's May 1863 talk at BAM. (See Chap. 3.)

in the presence of a great man mentally. I also made the discovery that it is much easier to see and converse with a great man than with a small man; with a big man than with a little one. [*Laughter and applause.*]

I found Mr. Lincoln seated in a low chair, and surrounded on all sides by unbound books and papers which I thought he had been overhauling.

Reception to Douglass.

I approached, he began to rise to receive me, and he continued to rise, higher and higher, till I found myself looking up to him and he looking down upon me. He gave me a welcome which was none too much, nor too little, but just enough to make me at ease.

First, I began to talk of myself, as I have been doing this evening. I told him what I had been doing. He blandly put an end to it all by saying: "Mr. Douglass, you need not tell me who you are. I know who you are. Mr. Seward has told me all about you." Brought thus to a standstill, I proceeded with the object of my visit.

I said: "Mr. President, I have been recruiting colored troops, and if you want me to succeed I must be able to assure them that colored soldiers, while in the service shall have pay equal to that of white soldiers; secondly, that when they shall perform acts of bravery in battle, which would secure promotion to white soldiers, the like promotion shall be accorded colored soldiers: thirdly, that if the threat of Jefferson Davis's carried out, you, President Lincoln, will retaliate in kind." [*Good! Good!*]

Feeling myself now perfectly free to say to Mr. Lincoln all that I thought on the subject, I supported my demands as best I could with arguments, to which he calmly and patiently listened, not once interrupting me, and when I had finished he made a careful reply, covering each proposition that I had submitted to him.

He admitted the justice of the demand for equal wages and equal promotion to colored soldiers, but reminded me that for the moment there were causes for delay in its execution. He called my attention to the necessity at that critical time, of avoiding any shock to the prejudices of the white soldiers, and told me of the many objections there were to making colored men soldiers; of the doubts entertained of them, of how it was first proposed that they should be employed simply as laborers; that they should be clothed in a peculiar and inferior uniform; that they should not bear arms, but that they should work in trenches with pick-ax and shovel; that, as time went on, they were thought worthy to be soldiers, but were not to take the field like other soldiers. They were only to hold fortified positions in sickly places, after those places should be captured by white soldiers. He thought it was a great thing that they could be armed and uniformed as soldiers at all. He held, however, that in time the first two points I had insisted upon would be conceded: that colored soldiers would be equally paid and equally promoted.

But when it came to the matter of retaliation, the tender heart of the president appeared in the expression of his eyes, and in every line of his care worn countenance, as well as in the tones of his appealing voice. "Ah!" said he, "Douglass, I cannot retaliate. I cannot hang men in cold blood. I cannot hang men who have had nothing to do with murdering colored prisoners. Of course, if I could get hold of the actual murderers of colored prisoners I would deal with them as they deserve, but I cannot hang those who had no hand in such murders." [*Applause.*] I was not convinced that Mr. Lincoln himself was right. [*Applause.*]

Enemies Loved Even in War.
I could, and did, answer Mr. Lincoln's arguments; but was silenced by his over-mastering mercy and benevolence. I had found a president with a heart—one who could, even in war, love his enemies; and that was something. In parting he said: "Douglass, never come to Washington without calling upon me." And I never did.

Though neither of the objects sought were immediately obtained I was full of faith in the man, and felt sure that he would do what he could to secure justice to our soldiers and protection to the lives of colored prisoners. I saw Mr. Lincoln several times after this interview, and found him ever the same large-hearted man as when I first met him. At one time during the war he sent for me to consult as to how to get more slaves into our line.[138] He had offered them freedom and protection, but he said that they were not coming in fast enough.

While we were talking over the matter, Governor [William] Buckingham, the [Republican] war governor of Connecticut [*applause*], was announced, and I at once arose and asked leave to withdraw, saying to Mr. Lincoln: "I must not stay to prevent your interview with Governor Buckingham." Instead of allowing me to leave, he said to the messenger, in his peculiarly high and honest voice: "Tell Governor Buckingham to wait. I am talking with my friend Douglass." [*Applause.*]

In this interview President Lincoln told me to devise some plan by which to get more slaves within our line, and to submit my plan to him. I did so; but it was never after to put the plan into operation. Our rapid successes, and the increasing intelligence of the slaves concerning the new departure of the loyal people and government in their favor, brought the freemen into our lines much faster than the means we had could care for them.

I have often said that Mr. Lincoln was the first great man with whom I could talk for hours without being once reminded, either by way of compliment or condescension, of my color.

Perhaps this statement was a little too strong; but it

---

138 This meeting occurred on August 19, 1864.

seemed true when I made it. The impression I designed to make was that Mr. Lincoln said and did nothing during our interview that reminded me in any way of our difference in color. He not only invited me to see him at the White House, but he invited me to tea with him at the Soldiers' Home [*applause*]; and convinced me that he was far above the prevailing prejudices of his countrymen.

I found Mr. Lincoln different from my expectation of him, not only in his kindness to me, but also in his manners, which were very different from the current representation of them. He had been described as wanting in dignity, as jocose, and fond of telling witty stories. This description of him doubtless has some foundation, for

> "A little nonsense, now and then.
> Is relished by the best of men."[139]

A Sadly Earnest Man.

But I am bound to say of President Lincoln that it was never my lot to find him in such mood. His whole deportment was a contradiction and a rebuke to everything like levity or merry-making. He was not only intensely in earnest but sadly in earnest. The dimmed light in his eye, and the deep lines in his strong American face, told plainly the story of the heavy burden of care

---

139 A nursery rhyme.

that weighed upon his spirit. I could as easily dance at a funeral as to jest in the presence of such a man. I feel that his heart was occupied with thought of his imperiled country and of its brave sons, imperiled and dying on the battlefield.

I was present at the beginning of President Lincoln's second term, and witnessed his second inauguration.[140] I saw and followed his carriage that day from the White House to the Capitol. Pennsylvania Avenue had not then felt the energy of Governor Shepherd.[141] It was a thoroughfare of mud. The wheels of Mr. Lincoln's carriage sank in it nearly to the hubs, and it was easy to keep pace with his horses. For some reason, or for no reason, I was oppressed with a dread foreboding as I followed his carriage. The fear was upon me that Mr. Lincoln might be shot down on his way to the Capitol, and it was a great relief to me when the trip was safely ended. I know not why, but I felt that there was murder in the air of Washington. No hint had then been given that in the dark places of the city, someone was seeking the life of Mr. Lincoln.

I stood near the steps of the east front of the Capitol when Mr. Lincoln appeared and had the oath of office administered to him by Chief Justice [Salmon

---

140 Lincoln's second inauguration was on March 4, 1865; he was assassinated on the night of April 14, and died the next day.

141 As Blassingame and McKivigan note (Vol. 5, p. 542), Douglass was referring to the significant civic improvements made in the capital city during the 1870s by Alexander Robey Shepherd, the "father of modern Washington, DC."

P.] Chase. I heard his remarkable, memorable, and, I might say, wonderful speech on that occasion. To me he seemed more the saint and prophet, in his appearance as well as in his utterance, than he did the president of a great nation, and the commander-in-chief of its army and navy. To understand that brief speech of Mr. Lincoln's we must remember that he had been fiercely and bitterly criticized from at least three different quarters. He had been assailed by Northern Democrats for making the war an abolition war. He had been denounced by the abolitionists for not making it an abolition war. He was denounced for not making peace at any price, and, again, for not prosecuting the war with more vigor. He answered all his critics with the following brief sentence: "Fondly do we hope, fervently do we pray that this mighty scourge of war will soon pass away. [*Applause.*] Yet, if God wills that it continue until all the wealth piled by the bondsman's two hundred and fifty years of unrequited toil shall be sunk, and until every drop of blood drawn by the lash shall be paid by another drawn by the sword, as was said three thousand years ago, so still it must be said. 'The judgements of the Lord are true and righteous altogether.'" [*Applause.*]

Lincoln Spoke As if Inspired.
This was said in a voice of deep solemnity, bordering upon inconsolable sadness; but a voice as firm as the ever lasting hills, and as pure and clear as the "brave old

overhanging sky."[142] There seemed at the time to be in the man's soul the united souls of all the Hebrew prophets. I was much relieved when the president returned in safety to his room, for I was, all through his speech, haunted with the thought that he might be murdered before he could finish what he had to say.

In the evening I attended Mr. Lincoln's inaugural reception. It was a new experience for Washington, a new experience for me, and a new experience for the country, to see a person like myself present on such an occasion. [*Applause.*]

I was once in Albany, in company with that princely philanthropist, the late Hon. Gerrit Smith, and was invited with him to dine with E.C. Delavan,[143] an eminent gentleman of that city. I was about declining to accept this invitation, when the great-hearted Gerrit Smith said: "Oh, yes, Douglass go! Someone must break the ice!" [*Laughter.*]

Well, I did go, and did break the ice, and have been breaking ice ever since [*laughter*] and some of it pretty hard and thick ice. Having witnessed the inauguration of Mr. Lincoln in the morning, my colored friends urged me to attend the inauguration reception at the executive mansion in the evening. Here, indeed, I found solid ice to break, for no man of my race, color or previous con-

142 Douglass is paraphrasing a line from *Hamlet* (see Blassingame and McKivigan, 543).
143 A leading figure in the temperance movement.

dition, had ever attended such a reception, except as a servant or waiter. I did not look upon the matter lightly, either subjectively or objectively. To me it was a serious thing to break in upon the established usage of the country, and run the risk of being repulsed; but I went to the reception, determined to break the ice, which I [did] in an unexpectedly rough way.

When my [companion and I] presented ourselves at the door of the White House we were met by two sturdy policemen, who promptly informed us that we could not be allowed to enter, and when we attempted to enter without their consent they pushed us back with some violence. I was, however, determined not to be repulsed and forced myself and lady inside the door, despite the guard. But my trouble was not ended by that advantage. A policeman inside met us and with a show of friendliness, said to us: "Oh, yes; come this way! come this way!" Thinking that he was about to conduct us to the famous East Room, where the reception was proceeding, we followed the lead of our new, red-faced, burly, blue-coated friend; but just when we thought that we were entering, we found ourselves being conducted through an outside window on a plank for the exit of the visitors. [*Laughter.*]

I never knew so exactly what was meant by walking the plank. [*Laughter.*] I said, "This will not do." To a gentleman who was passing at the moment I said, "Tell Mr. Lincoln that Frederick Douglass is at the door and is refused admission." I did not walk the plank, and, to the policeman's astonishment, was especially invited into the spacious East Room, and we found ourselves in a bewildering sea of beauty and elegance [*applause*], such as my poor eyes had never before seen in any one room at home or abroad. High above every other figure in the room, and overlooking the brilliant scene, stood the towering form of Mr. Lincoln, completely hemmed in by the concourse of visitors passing and taking his hand as they passed. The scene was so splendid, so glorious that I almost repented of my audacity in daring to enter.

"Here Comes My Friend Douglass."

But as soon as President Lincoln saw me I was relieved of all embarrassment. In a loud voice, so that all could hear, and looking toward me, he said, "And here comes my friend, Frederick Douglass!" [*Good! Good!*] I had some trouble in getting through the crowd of elegantly dressed people to Mr. Lincoln.

When I did succeed, and shook hands with him, he detained me and said, "Douglass, I saw you in the crowd today, listening to my inaugural address. How did you like it?" I replied, "Mr. Lincoln, I must not stop to talk now. Thousands are here, wishing to shake your hand." But he said, "You must stop. There is no man in the United States whose opinion I value more than yours. How did you like it?" [*Applause.*] I said, "Mr. Lincoln, it was a sacred effort," and passed on, amid some smiles, much astonishment and some frowns. And this was the last time that I heard the voice and saw the face and form of honest Abraham Lincoln.

A few weeks later he fell before the bullet of the assassin. His murder was the natural outcome of a war for slavery. He fell a martyr to the same barbarous and bloody spirit which now pursues, with outrage and vengeance, the people whom he emancipated and whose freedom he secured. Did his firm hand now hold the helm of state; did his brave spirit now animate the nation; did his wisdom now shape and control the destiny of this otherwise great republic; did he now lead the once-great Republican Party, we should not, as now, hear from the nation's capital the weak and helpless, the inconsistent humiliating confession that, while there are millions of money and ample power in the United States government to protect the lives and liberties of American citizens in the republics of Haiti and far-off Chile, and in every other foreign country on the globe, there is no power under the United States Constitution to protect the lives and liberties of American citizens in any one of our own Southern states from barbarous, inhuman and lawless violence.

Douglass's fervent appeal for protection of the Negroes in the South, delivered with all his old fire, brought the company to their feet with a burst of cheering.

POSTSCRIPT

In February 1963, as the fight for civil rights commanded the national spotlight, Reverend Martin Luther King Jr. visited Plymouth Church. There, in the historic Brooklyn redoubt of abolitionism frequented a century earlier by Frederick Douglass, King delivered "The American Dream," a preview of the landmark oration he would serve up that summer at the March on Washington. The nation faced no full-scale insurrection when King spoke, but deadly racist violence continued to stalk the land. Rather than a civil war, King told his audience, America was somewhat hypocritically presenting itself as a champion of freedom in the Cold War; meanwhile, anticolonial struggles like the one led by Mahatma Gandhi in India had provided inspiration for oppressed people across the globe. Yet even though the geopolitical picture may have been different, for black people in the United States a century after the Civil War, injustice remained entrenched. King, echoing Douglass, thus told his Plymouth audience that America was "a dream yet unfulfilled," with the reality of second-class citizenship contradicting the nation's founding principle of equality.

The Brooklyn visited by MLK during this era had nonetheless changed considerably from Douglass's day. By the mid-twentieth century, the African American population of the borough had grown exponentially, with Bedford-Stuyvesant beginning to rival Harlem as a black cultural capital. As in other Northern cities, midcentury redlining and disinvestment were creating distinct patterns of residential segregation in Brooklyn. In the later decades of the twentieth century, substantial migrations from Caribbean nations would also give Brooklyn one of the largest black populations in the United States. Amid the warp-speed gentrification of the borough in recent years, many black Brooklynites understandably feel threatened. Indeed, so many of the questions first raised by Douglass about black equality assume added resonance in today's "New" Brooklyn.

But like King, Douglass first and foremost must be understood as a product of his time. As an escaped slave, Douglass clearly understood the need for black people to secure their own freedom. Yet he was also keenly aware of the many impediments to ending slavery—whether white supremacy, the economic interests of Brooklyn and New York City merchants, or the reluctance of local and national politicians to challenge the South's power. Even so, as illustrated in the speeches here, Douglass never backed down in his fight for full black freedom. Upon his death in 1895, Theodore Tilton, Douglass's most enduring Brooklyn comrade, perhaps said it best:

Spake I of goodly giants in the land?
   And did I boast that I had known them well?
   I was a stripling: so I live to tell,
In these degenerate days, how great and grand,
How plain and simple, were the noble band
   Who cried to Heaven against that crime of Hell
   Which to the auction-block brought Babes to sell,
And which on Women burnt a market-brand!

Who were those heroes? Since the roll is known
   I need not call it: Lincoln was the chief:
   The rest were legion—name them whoso can:
But whoso counts the list of Freedom's Own
   Must name the Chattel whom, with pride and grief,
   We buried yesterday and called a Man![144]

---

144 Theodore Tilton, *Sonnets to the Memory of Frederick Douglass* (Paris, France: Brentano's, 1895).

Acknowledgments

As this project took shape, I benefited greatly from the help provided by a wide array of scholars and archivists. Jack McKivigan, project director and editor of the *Frederick Douglass Papers,* offered ample suggestions and furnished insightful feedback on my introduction. He also steered me to Douglass specialists including Robert Wallace and Celeste-Marie Bernier, who generously shared their support as well. Louis DeCaro Jr. helped answer many of my questions regarding Douglass's relationship with John Brown. Special thanks also go to Dr. Walter Evans, whose collection of nineteenth-century artifacts of black history includes many important Douglass materials.

My knowledge of Douglass's milieu grew immeasurably during my participation in "City of Print: New York and the Periodical Press," a 2015 NEH summer seminar held in Downtown Brooklyn under the direction of CUNY's Mark Noonan. Among many other participants, Gretchen Long, Adam McKible, Jennifer Moore, and Brian Sweeney gave me important research cues. I very much look forward to future collaborations with fellow City of Print alum Jim Casey, cocoordinator of the Colored Conventions project (coloredconventions.org), a treasure trove of nineteenth-century African American history.

I am indebted to a number of research librarians and their staffs, including Mariam Touba of the New York Historical Society and Maira Liriano and Shola Lynch at the Schomburg Center. Julie Golia of the Brooklyn Historical Society (BHS) also provided various essential materials—some of which came from the excellent BHS exhibition about abolitionism in Brooklyn on view until the winter of 2018 (pursuitoffreedom.org). The Brooklyn Collection of the Brooklyn Public Library (BPL) is also an indispensable resource for the study of local history. All of the *Brooklyn Daily Eagle* clippings contained in this volume can be found in the BPL's Brooklyn Newsstand (bklyn.newspapers.com).

T.H.
Sunset Park, Brooklyn
October 2016